Math Vitamins

Math Vitamins

Daily Dose for Students Learning How

to Solve Word Problems

Loretta Jean Everhart

iUniverse, Inc.
Bloomington

Math Vitamins
Daily Dose for Students Learning How to Solve Word Problems

iUniverse books may be ordered through booksellers or by contacting:

iUniverse
1663 Liberty Drive
Bloomington, IN 47403
www.iuniverse.com
1-800-Authors (1-800-288-4677)

Because of the dynamic nature of the Internet, any web addresses or links contained in this book may have changed since publication and may no longer be valid. The views expressed in this work are solely those of the author and do not necessarily reflect the views of the publisher, and the publisher hereby disclaims any responsibility for them.

Any people depicted in stock imagery provided by Thinkstock are models, and such images are being used for illustrative purposes only.
Certain stock imagery © Thinkstock.

ISBN: 978-1-4620-3251-8 (sc)
ISBN: 978-1-4620-3252-5 (ebk)

Printed in the United States of America

iUniverse rev. date: 08/16/2011

CONTENTS

Dedication

This book is dedicated to my parents, Russell and Mary Everhart. I am the person I am today because of their love and care.

Acknowledgements

There are some people I need to thank since this book would not have been started nor completed without their assistance, encouragement, teaching, and support.

First of all, I want to thank two of my math supervisors, Cleo Campbell and Anita Morris. Both encouraged me to grow as a teacher in elementary mathematics. Cleo Campbell taught the first class of lead math teachers in my county. I was fortunate and honored to have been in that class. Anita Morris initiated a math masters program for elementary school teachers. I had the pleasure of attending some of the classes she taught for that program.

Second, I want to thank Jennifer Taylor-Cox who not only taught my first course on differentiating instruction, but she also motivated me to expand what I already knew about math instruction and to write.

Third, I wish to thank my two proofreaders, Alice Newton and Heather Everhart. Both Alice and Heather shared their thoughts as parents on how the ideas in this book helped them understand how they can work with their own children in the area of problem solving skills. Heather also taught me how to use some of the tools on the word processor.

Finally, I wish to thank Alice Murphy for her words of encouragement throughout the creation of this book. Whenever I felt like giving up, she gave me the boost I needed.

Quote

"what a child can do today with assistance, she will be able to do by herself tomorrow."
Lev Vygotsky.

"I learned that the only way you are going to get anywhere in life is to work hard at it. Whether you're a musician, a writer, an athlete or a businessman, there is no getting around it. If you do, you'll win—if you don't you won't."
Bruce Jenner

Introduction

When I was teaching, I often found students who were quite literally nervous when problem solving time came. Some would even break out into sweats. I remember one little boy would have a faster heart beat when problem solving was even mentioned.

When I approached the parents for assistance, sometimes I found the same anxiety. Sometimes the anxiety came from their own experiences with solving math problems in school. Sometimes it came from not knowing what to do to help their children feel more comfortable.

Then last year I was a vendor at a home schooling convention where I met some parents who were concerned about how to help their children with problem solving.

Result? I wrote this book.

I wrote this book for:

Parents who:

• Home school their children
• Have children who need extra help in problem solving
• Want to give their children extra practice in solving word problems

Teachers who are:

• New to teaching
• New to teaching math
• Searching for some new ideas to improve their students' problem solving skills

What is a word problem?

A word problem is a story with numbers and words. This word problem might consist of one sentence or a whole page, and it could be simple or complex with multi-steps. Whatever the case might be, the word problem needs to be solved by the reader.

Is there a plan or model for solving word problems?

Actually, there are several, but this book uses Polya's 4 Step Model since so many teachers have been encouraged to use it. Some educators have taken parts of Polya's model and adapted them to meet the needs of their students and match what they teach in math class. Adapting something is what teachers do. Teachers have learned to take bits and pieces of various methods to create their own model.

In this book, there is a detailed explanation of Polya's model in Chapter 5. Since some strategies are stressed, there is one example for each strategy with an explanation. The Appendix contains many of the word problems mentioned for each strategy so teachers can create transparencies or write the problems on chart paper. These problems are meant to be starting points. They have been written for various levels, so teachers and parents need to choose which ones they can use as they are and which ones they need to adapt.

Chapter 8 deals with the issues causing math anxiety as well as some strategies to prevent it or lessen its severity. In Chapter 9, What To Do If Students Are Having Difficulty in Understanding Word Problems, there are suggestions for techniques that both teachers and parents can employ to assist children who are experiencing difficulty in reading and understanding the word problems, have limited verbal ability to explain their thinking, or have difficulty with "picturing" the problem story. Chapter 10 offers writing and reading strategies to help students further understand the art of problem solving. There are also chapters on Connections and Differentiating Instruction since both are crucial to students' success in problem solving. Strategies for cooperative learning are interspersed throughout the book.

In the Appendix, readers will find copies of Polya's problem solving model so they can make copies to pass out to students for their math binders, and create posters to place around the room. Making these posters or copies handy will encourage students to use the problem solving model. Having a problem solving model helps students be organized which is very important to solving problems.

What tools and materials might students use to solve the word problem? Depending upon the problem, they might need:

- calculator
- ruler
- pencil
- paper
- graph paper, preferably the kind with 1 cm squares

- manipulatives (which are not just for the primary grades)
- student's journal of other problems for comparison
- chart of a problem solving model
- math dictionary
- individual slates

Math Dictionary

Having a math dictionary is quite useful. Teachers and parents could purchase one or they could have their students construct one to keep in their math binders. Having students make one might be more beneficial since they will be including math terminology that they currently need with definitions and illustrations they understand. As new math terminology is introduced, the students could add the new words to their dictionary. This is explained in more detail in Chapter 3.

Journal

Having the students create a problem solving journal will give them an extra resource to use whenever they are facing difficult problems or when they forget how to solve problems similar to the ones they have done at an earlier time. This journal should contain a few examples of each problem solving skill that have been taught, but teachers should not expect the students to include every single problem they have solved. Maintaining a problem solving journal is further explained in Chapter 7.

Calculator

Sometimes the person solving the problem might be able to complete the calculations in his or her head. This is known as math intuition. However, when the problem constitutes large whole numbers, decimals, fractions, or multi-steps, solving the problem in one's mind may be too difficult or too time consuming.

Using a calculator can be helpful when the students are busy working on a complex problem. Suppose the students have a case study on planning a vacation to one of the states after a US geography unit. This trip would mean calculating gasoline mileage, miles to travel to various destinations, sightseeing places, amusement parks, food, hotels, and activities. The case study would include fees and prices for every place they will be going.

Sometimes the teacher might assign the students a problem that has a skill they have not yet learned such as using percentages for discounts in a sale, or the teacher might assign a case study where very large numbers are involved such as the distances from Earth to the other planets and the Sun. Since the main point here is problem solving, the teacher can choose to have the students use calculators, but they still need to show their work or write an explanation on how they solved each part of their studies or projects.

Manipulatives

Manipulatives are not just for the young students in primary grades. Any student from grades Pre-Kindergarten through eight should be permitted to have access to a variety of items that can be manipulated as students are figuring out solutions. Having hands-on items for representing concepts is very important to developing understanding.

For geometry, logic, and patterns, students should have access to tangrams, pattern blocks, color chips, pentominoes, 3-D shapes, and square tiles. They could even use Post it notes and toothpicks! For measurement, the students should have access to measuring tapes, rulers, scales, measuring spoons, and clocks. The teacher should maintain a variety of items some place convenient for counting as well as practicing adding, subtracting, multiplying, and dividing. Fraction pieces as well as manipulatives that will help students visualize decimals and percentages are important. Teacher Resources and Nasco are just two of the companies that offer a variety of manipulatives.

The teacher should designate a special place in the class to keep these manipulatives convenient. A sign out system could be employed, and perhaps a student could be in charge of maintaining this special area. Parents can do the same at home.

Computers

Teachers should search for a variety of programs that can be used to help children learn more about problem solving. Some programs even have students run simulations such as creating a lemonade stand or an amusement park. There are so many interesting and fun websites that encourage students to explore various math concepts. Some sites even allow students to "move" tangrams and other manipulatives to solve problems. Sudoku puzzles and jigsaw puzzles are available for students of all levels. These websites allow students to explore solving problems without fear of making mistakes.

In the Appendix, there is a list of various websites that both teachers and parents can either use with children or find more information on problem solving activities. However, students should not be looking for these sites by themselves. Parents and teachers should preview these sites first.

Individual slates

Slates are great tools for students to show the teachers or their parents what they know and need to learn. During a lesson on examining word problems more closely, the children write down the information that is needed to solve the problem, extra information included in the same problem, or what is needed, but missing from the problem. Then the students could hold up their slates to show what they have written. As the teacher glances around the room, he/she can spot rather quickly who is grasping the concept and who needs some more work. Practice like this can continue with other word problems.

"The real process of education should be the process of learning to think through the application of real problems." John Dewey

Chapter 1

Why Teach Problem Solving Skills

Today's world utilizes mathematics continuously. When people determine which purchase to make or which car insurance or a health plan would best meet their needs and price range, they are implementing their math skills. A vast assortment of mathematical information can be located whenever the Internet, CD-ROMs, and other media are used. In the workplace, the level of mathematical thinking and problem solving has increased dramatically.

Those who understand and can implement mathematical skills correctly will have opportunities that others do not. The level of a person's mathematical competence opens doors to productive futures. A lack of mathematical competence closes those same doors.

Children need to be able to solve word problems for the following reasons:

- To see the need to learn new math skills
- To apply recently taught math skills independently
- To improve their willingness to try problems and gain determination in looking for solutions
- To independently apply math skills in solving real world problems that directly affect them
- To solve these problems all through adult life
- To pass entrance exams for the military, civil service, college, or vocational schools
- To be able to transfer this problem solving skill in other facets of life
- To reduce the chance of math anxiety

Seeing the need to learn new math skills

How often have teachers heard their students or their own children ask, "Why do we need to learn this?" It is a valid question. Unfortunately, it often goes unanswered. When that happens, students tend to shut down or lose interest in the learning process.

When teachers and parents introduce a new math skill or a series of related math skills, they should present to the students a word problem or offer a scenario where those skills could be employed. Children tend to learn better when they realize why they need the skill or skills. They need a goal to work towards. They need to hear why skills and concepts are important, but they need to hear the explanation in terms that they would understand and appreciate. That is the main reason why teachers are now required in so many school districts to include objectives in their daily schedules on the wall or chalkboard.

The math problem or case study could be placed on chart paper or somewhere on the chalkboard. It should be kept there as the various related math skills are being taught. Then, when those series of skills have been successfully mastered, the class can analyze and solve that problem. Basically, the children are seeing the big picture or goal. Seeing the big picture motivates children.

Applying skills recently taught

The best way to find out if the students have learned the recently taught skills is to assign children word problems after each set of new skills. Any difficulties during such problem solving activities can be diagnosed and the skills could be remediated. Below are some questions that can guide the teachers during this process.

- Do students understand and use the correct math vocabulary?
- Can they perform the math skill independently?
- Can they orally explain how they solved the problem?
- Are they able to write about their solution?

One of the reasons many children have difficulty with solving word problems is that they do not understand and use the correct math terminology. As soon as children begin to read, they can begin to work on math. That is when they should start learning math vocabulary. More information on developing vocabulary for mathematics is further developed in Chapter 3.

If the math skill itself is still presenting some difficulty, then the teacher needs to reteach that skill or review the skill periodically. Teachers might need to employ a different method of teaching the skill. They need to remember many children, even **older** students, need hands-on activities for learning math concepts. During lesson planning, it is important to keep in mind that some students might catch onto new concepts more quickly than some of the other students. Sometimes teachers can use the students who are doing well with the new concept as assistants and assign them to groups who need extra help. Teachers could also use learning centers that contain challenging word problems for the students who finish early so the teachers can further instruct the students experiencing difficulty with the new concepts.

Teachers need to be aware of each student's learning style, strengths, and skills. That knowledge should be used to differentiate some lessons. Teachers might need to consider assigning differentiated homework so the students who understood the concepts can do challenging projects while the other students can work on review activities.

Oral explaining on how students solve the problems

How often should the students explain orally? Explaining orally how to solve a problem could be done when a new skill has been taught. Perhaps the students could explain aloud after having had some practice with a particular word problem skill.

The class could even be divided into small groups where each group is assigned a different problem for the oral explanation time. This offers students the opportunity to hear their classmates' viewpoints on why they solved the problem a certain way. Working together on oral explanations can help the students understand and evaluate their classmates' processes for thinking, which in turn can improve their own style of explaining. How? The students might hear an important detail or point that they forgot. The students could even be permitted to choose which problem they want to explain aloud rather than assign them a certain problem out of the ones they are doing. Children like having choices.

Another time for explaining aloud would be when a particular student is having some difficulty with the work. Often, having the student explain aloud what they did to solve the problem can help the teacher locate the student's difficulty with the skill. However, the students should not be explaining aloud every single word problem. Besides being time consuming, this would cause overload and loss of interest in math.

Why is the oral explanation important, particularly with the younger children? Oral explanation offers the teacher the opportunity to hear how well the concepts being used are understood by the students. Quite often children can solve an easy word problem and have no idea how they did it. They are simply mirroring what they have seen others do, not comprehending what is going on. Oral explanation from a child offers the teacher or parent the opportunity to diagnose any difficulty the child might be experiencing with problem solving.

When children are able to explain the whys and hows, then perhaps understanding is really setting in. Also, when children share their solutions and reasons for choosing the strategy, learning is strengthened. They develop a stronger mathematics vocabulary which is key for understanding the lessons. Oral explanation is extremely important in leading children into the written explanation.

Teachers need to model oral explanations each time they teach a different math skill as well as each time they teach a different strategy for solving word problems. Whenever a new math skill or a different problem solving strategy is being introduced, the teacher could also be introducing new math terminology. For example, guess and test strategy involves different vocabulary than using the strategy, logic. If explaining orally about solving the problem is presenting the class with some difficulty, then the class should practice math talk. As the teacher and students are working on math skills, they need to use the math vocabulary associated with the skills being taught. Math talk needs to become as natural as kicking the ball.

Modeling how to orally explain the solution to the problem

Mrs. Harris was teaching her son, Bobby, how to solve word problems. Bobby was having some difficulty in explaining aloud how to solve one of the word problems. So Mrs. Harris modeled for her son how to explain orally.

Mrs. Harris: Bobby read the word problem.

Sammy the Squirrel was collecting nuts. He had gathered five peanuts, four acorns, and six walnuts. How many nuts did Sammy have?

Mrs. Harris: Bobby, retell the problem in your own words.

Bobby: The squirrel had 4 acorns. He found 5 peanuts. And he also found 6 walnuts.

Mrs. Harris: What is the problem asking us to do?

Bobby: We need to find out how many nuts the squirrel has.

Mrs. Harris: Show me how you would find the answer.

Bobby wrote 5 + 4 + 6 = 15.

Mrs. Harris: 15 what?

Bobby wrote nuts after 15.

Mrs. Harris: Bobby, listen to me carefully as I explain aloud how you solved this problem.

Mrs. Harris: The squirrel had 3 kinds of nuts. I added 5 peanuts, 4 acorns, and 6 walnuts to get a total of 15 nuts. I added because the problem asked for how many nuts the squirrel had.

Mrs. Harris: Now you explain aloud how you solved this problem.

Bobby: I added 5, 4, and 6 to get 15 nuts. I added because the problem asked how many.

Mrs. Harris: Very good Bobby.

Bobby did not repeat verbatim what his mother said. That is certainly okay so long as Bobby demonstrated an understanding of the problem, which he did. What if Bobby could not explain how to solve the problem even after his mother did? Sometimes modeling might need to be incorporated in the lessons a few times before the students can orally explain independently. If the student was not able to copy the explanation, then the modeling should be demonstrated again.

For the next few word problems, the teacher should model how to explain orally. Afterwards the students repeat what was said. Modeling is a great teaching tool that adults have been using for teaching many other things such as using manners, eating dinner, dressing, passing in papers, walking in lines, and so on.

Why should students write in math class? Writing should be an essential part of teaching in all subjects. Writing an explanation is an effective method for helping students think about ideas. However, progress has been slow in the area of writing in mathematics. Why? Mathematics is seen as a subject that communicates through the manipulation of symbols in orderly ways, not as one that uses words to express ideas. This view is unfortunate and misleading.

The process of writing requires gathering, organizing, and clarifying thoughts. It demands finding out what is known and what is not known. It calls for thinking clearly. The process of doing mathematics depends on gathering, organizing, and clarifying thoughts, finding out what is known and unknown, and thinking clearly. The final representation of mathematics may look different from the writing product, but the process of obtaining the final products is very similar.

What if the students are having difficulty with writing the explanation? Once again the teacher needs to model it. The class could solve a word problem together. The students could explain to a partner how to solve the problem. Then the teacher models how to write an explanation. This modeling might need to be repeated a few times before the children can write their own explanation independently. Using their vocabulary section for assistance in spelling and choosing the right words should be permitted. Being patient is important here. Being able to explain how to solve word problems is not easy for many children.

Modeling writing the explanation

Mrs. Harris and Bobby are working on another word problem. Although Bobby is now able to explain aloud how to solve word problems, he is having some difficulty in writing the explanation. So his mother is modeling or showing Bobby an example.

Mrs. Harris: Bobby, read the word problem aloud.

In September, the fourth grade had a book-reading contest. Steven read 9 books, Allen read 5, Cierra read 8, Kristen read 11, Mary read 3, and Marcus read 6. Who read the most books, the girls or the boys?

Mrs. Harris: Okay, now I want you to solve this word problem.

Bobby first highlighted what he thought were the key words-Steven 9, Allen 5, Cierra 8, Kristen 11, Mary 3, Marcus 6

He also highlighted girls, boys, and most in the question.

This is his work.

Boys-Steven, Allen, Marcus 9 + 5 + 6 = 20

Girls-Cierra, Kristen, Mary 8 + 11 + 3 = 22

22—20 = 2 books

Mrs. Harris: Great work! Now we need to write how you solved the word problem.

Think about what you did first. Why? Now think about what you did with the numbers. Why?

Bobby: I listed the boys and then the girls so I can keep track of the number of boys and of girls. Then I wrote down how many books each child read. I added 9, 5, and 6 to see how many books the boys read. Then I added 8, 11, and 3 to see how many books the girls read. Since the question asked who read the most, the girls or the boys, I subtracted 20 from 22. Most usually means to subtract. The girls read 2 more books than the boys.

Mrs. Harris: Let's write what you just said.

Mrs. Harris wrote that Bobby listed the boys and girls separately so he could keep track of the books each group read. Then he put down how many books each child read. To find out how many books the boys read, he added 9, 5, and 6. To find out how many books the girls read, he added 8, 11, and 3. He added each time because he needed to find out how many books each group read. Then he took the two numbers and subtracted 20 from 22 since the question had asked who read the most. In other words, the question was comparing the two groups.

Mrs. Harris: Do you understand what I wrote? Any questions?

Bobby: Yes, Mom, I understand. It is pretty much what I had just said isn't it?

Mrs. Harris: Yes it is. Bobby, you can either write what I wrote or write in your own words how you solved the problem.

Bobby: Mom, I think I will write what you wrote this time.

At this point, Mrs. Harris could have had Bobby restate what she wrote to make sure he understood all of the words. Perhaps with the next word problem, Bobby will feel more comfortable to write in his own words.

Improving children's willingness and determination to work on word problems

An important goal for both teachers and parents is to make sure children become willing and determined to solve word problems. These two characteristics become important to all subjects in school as well as all facets of life. Improving children's willingness to work on word problems can be tricky. When the word problems are too easy or follow the same pattern frequently, the children become complacent because they can solve these problems with little effort. Then when the problems become more complicated, the children admit defeat because they never learned to continue looking for clues and become determined to solve the problem. Behavior problems can occur since the students feel defeated and even deflated. If the assigned word problems are too difficult, then perhaps students will be discouraged and concede before they even write their name on the paper. Once again, behavior problems can occur with no learning happening.

Teachers and parents need to find a good balance of easy, moderate, and difficult problems for the children to solve. For a particular math page or worksheet, the teacher determines which problems all of the students must complete. Then the students can decide which of the others they want to solve.

Another way to encourage students to work on math problems is to permit them to work in pairs on some of the assignments. Working with a partner can alleviate some of the math anxiety children often feel. All of the students need to learn that they can solve problems on their own, and they need to know that they will not always have a team or a partner. However, working with a partner or in teams when a new skill is introduced can help increase the students' comfort zone. Using partners or teams can also facilitate learning when case studies or more involved problems are assigned.

The lesson could be differentiated by assigning certain problems to the students who are below average, then a few to the students on grade level, and then the more difficult problems to the students who need the challenge. Next, the teacher could allow time for the students to share their solutions. Afterwards, the teacher could have the students choose which problems from each level of difficulty to solve.

Children can relate better to word problems if they deal with themes such as:

- Planning a family feast for a holiday
- Planning a birthday party
- Creating their own amusement park
- Writing word problems related to sports
- Planning a class trip
- Saving money for a favorite hobby or game and finding a "job" to earn money

Whenever possible, math should be fun and interesting. Teachers might try brainstorming for a variety of ideas on how the school can make math fun for everyone. Parents who are home schooling children might want to work with other parents doing the same in order to brainstorm how math can be fun and interesting.

Below are some ideas.

Write riddles for students to solve. Allow the students to write their own riddles and share with the class. Students could even share these math riddles with students from other schools in their area or from other states sort of like pen pals but instead riddle pals. These riddles could be posted on a wall so all of the students can refer to them and attempt to solve them. Perhaps fifth graders could read their riddle over the PA system for everyone to solve.

Students could draw pictures using only numbers. Or they could create a design using various shapes and some color. Actually some famous artists have done this. The students could even research these artists and study their art work. Then they could create their own masterpieces.

Game boards could be designed and constructed, and cards with problems could be created. The game boards and the die could help students understand probability as well as geometric shapes and measurement. As the students learn various skills, they could add cards with problems for their games. This could lead into a great review at the end of the school year when there seems to be a lot of down time during preparations for school closing.

Teachers and students could read books dealing with math and then discuss those books. One activity would be to read "Grandfather Tang" to students in the beginning of a geometry unit. This is a story about a Chinese grandfather telling his grandchild a story using tangrams to create animals. The students could write their own story and draw pictures using tangrams. Afterwards, the students could share their picture books with the lower grades. With this activity, language arts and math are being connected. Also, the students are working on spatial skills when they use the tangrams to create objects. Both the adults and the students could research tangrams on the Internet to learn more about using them.

Schools can help students appreciate math by having Family Math Night. Parents and their children are invited to come to school at night to solve a variety of problems. Some of these problems could be related to science and social studies to demonstrate how math is interconnected to other subjects. Include the art, music, and physical education teachers by having them create activities related to their subject. Involve the media specialist by having books with math as the theme ready to be shared or even acted out by the older students.

Following is a list of books dealing with Family Math Night.

Family Math Night Math Standards in Action by Jennifer Taylor-Cox, Ph.D., 2005, Eye on Education Inc. ISBN 1-930556-99-3

Mega-Fun Math Fairs Ideas and Activities by Susan Staylor, 2003, Carson-Dellosa Publishing Co Inc. ISBN 0-88724-974-4

Family Math by Jean Kerr Stemark, Virginia Thompson, and Ruth Cossey, 1986, Lawrence Hall of Science ISBN 0-912511-06-0

Schools could sponsor a Math Fair which can help students showcase their problem solving work and progress in learning difficult concepts. Math Fairs could be competitive or noncompetitive, depending upon the goals of the individual schools. Groups of home schooling parents can certainly hold math fairs. The math fair should have the following standards showcased:

- Number and Operations
- Algebra
- Geometry
- Measurement
- Data Analysis

A showcase or bulletin board that is seen by everyone could demonstrate a math theme each month. One theme could be using pictures of famous people with captions explaining how math is related to what they do. Themes showing graphs of all kinds could be displayed. A bulletin board about weather could be displayed with all kinds of mathematical data which could be changed day to day depending upon the latest weather update. A number line showing counting by 2s, 3s, or 5s could be set up in the hallway.

On National Pie Day in March, the whole school could celebrate with measuring the circumference, diameter, and radius of various circles. Some of these circles could be samples of food. Perhaps the cafeteria could even serve round foods such as hamburgers, carrot rounds, ice cream cups, and other foods that are circular. Students could draw pictures of these items and write captions. A display of this work could be placed where others can see. The school could invite parents in to be part of the celebration.

A kite day in March could be sponsored by the school. Before this special day, teachers could spend time in science and math classes to help students learn about the history of kites, the physic principles supporting the flight of the kites, and math skills needed to construct kites. The older students could work with the younger students to create the kites or share reports about kites. Some of the kite construction could be done in class while the remaining work could be done at home. Parents could be invited to come in for that special day. Perhaps the last 1½ hours of the school day could be devoted to actual kite flying.

Sudoku could be celebrated by having a contest in class. Teachers could assign their students age appropriate puzzles to solve. They check to see if the students can find a strategy for solving the Sudoku problems, or the teachers could have a Sudoku party where students can bring in a favorite snack and solve Sudoku puzzles.

Fourth and fifth graders could be involved in the game, *24*. Each card has 4 numbers, and the students have to figure out a way to use those 4 numbers to equal 24. The students are practicing their math facts with addition, subtraction, multiplication, and division as well as problem solving. In Anne Arundel County, Maryland, elementary schools sponsor a math competition featuring the game, *24*.

If a school is close to The National Security Agency, known as the NSA, that school could invite one of their speakers to come to the school. NSA wants to encourage children to become interested in math. They have a series of activities that they can share with students. If a school is not near the NSA, then perhaps that school can look up their website for information on math activities.

Students could investigate how different careers use math. In this way, the students can learn how truck drivers, carpenters, painters, doctors, businesses, chefs, and athletes use mathematics in their field of work.

Teachers and parents can help students see how math is important to all subjects. Math can be part of each science and social studies units. Math can even be part of the end of the unit projects. Integrating math with other subjects is very important so children can realize math is not just an isolated subject. Seeing how important math is can help students become more determined to solve their word problems.

Applying math skills independently to solve real world problems that directly affect them

The teachers and parents should make sure they use real world problems with children. Each year, children could be involved in planning a birthday party or planning a breakfast. Even a shopping outing can be a great way to show how important solving word problems can be.

In class, students could pretend they earn a weekly allowance of a certain amount of money. Part of the assignment would include the students deciding what to save their allowance for such as a game, a CD, a DVD, and other items that interest them. Then the teacher could assign them the task of looking up that special item in catalogs or the news ads for different places to buy it. Part of the assignment could be to find the best buy by comparing prices. The students could also keep track of their money each week and figure out how much more they need to save in order to buy that item. Each week, an adult could check with the students to see how much more they needed to save. The students should be required to explain orally how they figured that out. Can the students determine how many weeks they need to save their money before they have enough to buy the game?

Planning a vacation related to a unit of study

Children could plan a vacation that would correspond to a place of history or geography that they are studying. Writing letters to the tourist bureaus of various states or vacation spots for information and prices could be part of this unit. For example, Mrs. Potter's class was studying about caves during their science unit on earth science. As part of an end of unit activity, Mrs. Potter had her students plan a vacation to Luray Caverns in Virginia. The students wrote letters to Luray Caverns to learn more about the caverns as well as the prices for touring the place. They also had to include costs for traveling expenses, eating out, and sleeping arrangements. For extra credit, they could include another tourist attraction with this assignment.

Preparing children for solving math problems all through adult life

This part is particularly for parents although many teachers often showed their own students how they have used problem solving skills for their private life. Students could interview their parents on how they used problem solving at home, such as figuring how much tile to buy for a kitchen floor, size of bedspreads needed for each bed, and how much food should be purchased for a Thanksgiving feast.

Children need to see adults actively involved in solving mathematical problems for everyday life if they are going to see the importance of learning how to solve word problems. Involving their children whenever possible in realistic problem solving activities is important for developing appreciation for learning math skills. When parents give examples on how they might use mathematics, whether it be at home or at work, they help math become more meaningful.

Parents should **involve** their children with these math projects at home whenever possible. First they can involve the children by asking them questions about what the parents are doing. Then they should involve the children by asking them to locate items such as the measuring spoons and the ¾" screw. As their children mature, the parents can involve them in some of the planning and even doing part of the projects. Children feel important when they find the tools, become part of the planning, and actually take part in the projects.

Thinking aloud also helps children learn to think about solving problems. Parents help their children when they explain out loud answers to questions such as —What? When? How much? How often? Which tool or which item to use? Where?

Passing entrance exams

More and more, entrance exams to the military, civil service, college, vocational school and others consists of word problems. Future employers and schools want to know how well children can think and work through problems. Giving children a sound foundation in solving word problems can help them on these tests. If they have a workable problem solving model in their mind, they can use it without even realizing it. Using the model becomes second nature because the children have used it so frequently in their school years. Although these tests require higher math skills, the teacher in elementary school, or the parent who is either giving extra practice or home schooling, have all given children the mental tool to proceed with confidence.

Reducing the chance of math anxiety

Children encounter math anxiety when they have any difficulty in learning and applying math skills. Math anxiety is a real dilemma that many children and even adults face every day. Immersing the children in the world of problem solving helps students learn that they can apply their math skills, see the reasons why they should learn and master various math skills, and understand how math is connected to the real world. However the key is to immerse the children in math word problems that are not beyond their scope of understanding.

Transferring problem solving skills in other facets of life

Having good problem solving skills is quite advantageous in many situations. People who are good problem solvers do better in finding jobs, maintaining jobs, and gaining leadership roles. If one has a method of solving problems, that person can plan on solutions for situations at home, on vacation, while shopping, at work, and more. Problem solving skills can open doors of opportunities.

"What the mind can conceive, it can achieve." Napoleon Hill

Chapter 2

Getting Started

When parents start reading aloud to their children, they have one of the best opportunities to start involving them in solving math word problems. The library is full of books with math as a theme.

One example is *Five Little Monkeys Jumping on the Bed* by Eileen Christelow with the ISBN of 978-0-395-90023-9. This is a fun book to read aloud to young children. One book review said it was "pure silliness—just the kind kids like." ALA Booklist. Well, it is silly, but it also deals with math in a delightful way. The story starts with 5 monkeys jumping on the bed. Each time one falls off the bed. The story ends when there are no more monkeys jumping on the bed.

This is the perfect book for introducing subtraction to a young child in a word problem way. After reading it once through with no interruptions, the parent or another adult should reread it. They should encourage the child to retell the story as he looks at the pictures. The adults could even give the child 5 blocks to represent the monkeys as the child retells the story. When the child use the blocks, he is using one of the strategies for solving a word problem.

The next step would be asking the child questions about the story's math. How many monkeys were jumping on the bed in the beginning? How many monkeys were jumping on the bed at the end of the story? What happened to the monkeys? Not only is the child working on his comprehension of the story, but he is also working on his math skills.

Another technique would be to assign a drawing picture activity that would illustrate what is happening to the monkeys as they fall off the bed. Afterwards, the child should explain what the picture is showing. By having the child draw a picture, he is using another strategy for solving word problems.

Reread these books as often as possible. Ask questions about the story itself as well as the math involved with the story. Involve children in a discussion. Encourage them to retell the story using the pictures. Whenever possible allow children to use manipulatives to retell the story. The retelling is helping children work on their oral skills as well as work on visualizing what is happening. Both are important to reading and math. During the reading and discussing of these books, children are learning that math is connected to reading. Seeing how mathematics is connected to other subjects is extremely important because it helps children understand that math is not an isolated subject.

Examples of some books that have problem solving as the theme are included here. This is just a beginning list since there are many more. These books can be located on Amazon.com, in various book stores, and in the public library.

Spaghetti and Meatballs For All! by Marilyn Burns, Scholastic Paperbacks (August 1, 2008), ISBN—978-0545044455

One Hundred Hungry Ants by Elinor J. Pinczes, Houghton Mifflin Company (1993), ISBN—0-395-97123-3

Anno's Mysterious Multiplying Jar by Masaichiro Anno, Penguin Putnam Books for Young Readers (March 15, 1999), ISBN—978-0698117532

Amanda Bean's Amazing Dream by Cindy Neuschwander, Scholastic Press (August 1, 1998), ISBN—978-0590300124

Alexander, Who Used to Be Rich Last Sunday by Judith Viorst, Athenum (August 30, 1987), ISBN—978-0689711992

The Penny Pot (Math Start 3) by Stuart J. Murphy, HarperCollins, ISBN—978-0064467179

Grapes of Math by Greg Tang, Scholastic Paperbacks, ISBN—978-0439598408

Math Curse by Jon Scieszka, Viking Juvenile (October 1, 1995), ISBN—978-

0670861941

The King's Chessboard by David Birch, Puffin Books (July 1, 1993), ISBN—978-0140548808

One Grain of Rice: A Mathematical Folktale by Demi, Scholastic Press (April 1, 1997), ISBN—978-0590939980

The Toothpaste Millionaire by Jean Merrill, Sandpiper (September 4, 2006), ISBN—978-0618759255

Another interesting way to start working on problem solving in the early stage is to have jigsaw puzzles for the students to work on. Jigsaw puzzles can be useful to teach guess and test, which is a problem solving strategy. Use a puzzle with 100 pieces or less. Lay out the puzzle pieces. If this is the first time the students are working on puzzles, just let them have fun fitting the pieces together. After the puzzle was finished, have the students look carefully over the pieces and the picture on the box at the same time. Can they spot the puzzle pieces that resemble certain parts of the picture? Do they know where to place the pieces with a straight edge? Do they try to organize their pieces or do they work randomly?

As they solve different puzzles, parents need to ask the children what might help them find the right pieces in an easier and faster fashion. At first, do not make the purpose of this activity obvious, but keep modeling how to organize the puzzle pieces until the children start doing it on their own. Do not try to model everything right away. Do it gradually.

Model how to organize the puzzle pieces. What happens when children sort the pieces by straight edges? What happens when children sort by corner pieces? What happens when children sort by color or by looking at the picture on the box?

One teacher introduced her third grade students to jigsaw puzzles. After a bit of time on one particular puzzle, she would divide the class into groups of 4. Each group received a puzzle with no more than 100 pieces. Next she asked the groups the same questions that had just been previously suggested. Then the teacher assigned each group the task of finding a strategy for finishing the puzzle. Before the students started the activity, she stressed that she was not after which group was the fastest, but which group had a good plan.

After giving the groups some time to work together, the teacher then incorporated cooperative learning for discussing what each group did during this activity. The strategy she used is known as **Numbered Heads Together** which was mentioned in the Introduction of this book. Each student was assigned a number from 1-4. They did not know which number she would be calling out when it was time to explain their method for solving the puzzle. Therefore, they had to make sure everyone in the group understood the method and would be able to explain it clearly to the class.

Next, the teacher would give each group chart paper and a marker so they could record their strategy. After some preparation time, she then had one student from each group share their strategy with the class by calling one of the numbers from 1-4. The child assigned that particular number would stand up in class and wait to be called upon. Meanwhile, everyone is listening to each group's strategy. Sometimes, the teacher would call on someone from another group to rephrase what the speakers were saying to ensure that everyone was listening. At the end, each group basically figured out how to use a problem solving strategy called guess and test where the guesses were educated ones, not necessarily random ones.

Teachers and parents should involve children in games that incorporate concentrating, remembering, counting, and sequencing. Some games for the young children even involve money. When the family plays games like Monopoly, the younger ones can play with an adult or an older child. Games are fun, but they also teach skills. Having game night where the whole family can play a variety of games is a great idea for family togetherness as well as learning problem solving skills.

"It's key that students develop a firm understanding of mathematical concepts before learning new vocabulary, so that they can anchor terminology in their understanding." Marilyn Burns

Chapter 3

Developing a Mathematics Vocabulary

What does research say about vocabulary? Vocabulary can help students expand their knowledge which in turn helps them raise achievement in all subjects. In other words, the more words students know, the more they can learn, because students must know 95% of the words they are reading in order to comprehend spoken or written words.

Learning new words is a process in increments. Sometimes a brief lesson just before or after reading is enough for students to develop word understanding. A recommendation by Capps (1989) is to give students at least 6 exposures to a new word during the initial lesson and at least 30 other experiences during the following month. New and/or difficult math vocabulary should be repeated frequently in meaningful ways in order for students to retain and use those words correctly and often.

There are three levels of word knowledge. They are unknown, acquainted, and established (Beck and McKeown 1991, as cited by Lapp, Flood, and Farnan 1996 and Ryder and Graves 2003). What are **unknown** words? They are words that children can neither identify nor comprehend. These words have absolutely no meaning to the children. Consequently, they cannot understand the concepts using those words.

What are **acquainted** words? They are words that students may recognize because they have seen them or heard them before. However, they must consciously think about those words in order to recall what they mean. The children might be able to understand the page they are reading or the teacher's lesson, but more than likely, they will not be able to master the skills.

What are **established** words? These words are easily recognized and understood. The goal for mathematical vocabulary is for the terms to become established. Once the words have become established, students can then use those words while thinking, speaking, and writing in math class. Learning takes place and mastery of skills are possible. However, a word cannot become established with just one exposure.

Do students understand and use the correct math terminology? One of the reasons many children have difficulty with solving word problems is that they do not understand and use the correct math terminology. As soon as children begin to read, they begin to work on math. That is when parents and teachers should begin to help them learn math vocabulary.

Why is learning math vocabulary difficult for many students? Materials in mathematics are very difficult to read. There are more concepts per sentence and per paragraph. Therefore, it is extremely important to emphasize vocabulary instruction in math class.

There are four basic types of vocabulary in math. They are technical, subtechnical, symbolic, and general. Technical vocabulary is difficult and almost impossible to describe in everyday language. Technical words such as integer and quadrilateral have only one meaning that is specific to math. Often they are defined by using other technical terms which makes them even more difficult to learn.

Subtechnical vocabulary has more than one meaning which differs from one subject to another. The students may know one meaning of the subtechnical vocabulary word, but it might not be the one needed in math. For example, volume in science means how loud a sound is whereas in math it is the volume inside a cube. Sometimes a subtechnical word in math can even have more than one meaning. For instance, the word degree has different meanings from number of degrees in an angle to how hot it is.

Symbolic vocabulary contains the numerous symbols in mathematics. Symbols such as = + 1 < > are just a few examples of symbolic words that do not contain any parts of the alphabet.

General vocabulary would be the words used in everyday language. Quite often these words are found in the directions, explanations, and word problems. Seldom are they found in the glossary of the math text.

Teachers and parents do not necessarily have to learn about the four types of vocabulary, but they do need to be aware that vocabulary instruction in mathematics is not an easy task. The glossary in the math text can be used, but keep in mind the definitions often contain words that are difficult to understand because technical and subtechnical words are frequently part of the definitions.

Three things will help vocabulary learning increase. When students can attach a mental image to a word, they tend to understand the word. Also, when students are given the opportunity to categorize words into groups, they can employ that to attach further meaning and clarification. Being able to create labels is a useful tool for promoting new awareness of word meanings. For example, when a teacher introduces addition, students should label the parts of an addition problem in order to learn the terms. However, some specialists believe it takes a minimum of 15 encounters for students to learn the word and be able to use that word independently orally and in written form. Others believe students need at least 30 exposures to the word before the child can use it effectively and correctly.

Suggestions for teachers and parents teaching math vocabulary:

1. Utilize manipulatives whenever possible to teach concepts and vocabulary. Students do not need to be in the primary grades for manipulatives to be valuable. As the students utilize the manipulatives, the teachers and parents need to guide the math talk session. Students could even draw pictures of the terms while using the manipulatives.

2. Examine carefully the wording of the book for any new words or words that might be confusing to the students. Perhaps there are technical or subtechnical words that can be used as organizers. Also, there may be general words and even symbols that might interfere with learning if the students do not know or understand the meanings. Pre-teaching these words before the actual math lesson can possibly prevent confusion and lack of learning.

3. Utilize the students' real-world experiences to help them learn the concepts and new vocabulary. For example, looking for geometric shapes at home or even examples of how parents use fractions can be of tremendous help in assisting the students master the words.

4. Activate prior knowledge of the students with stronger math skills and working in groups to discuss what words mean can help those students with little or no prior experiences.

5. Model the use of math vocabulary when interacting with students which can lead to students learning those terms. For example, when the teachers use terms such as sum, product, difference, and quotient, rather than the word, answer, the students will see the importance of such words and learn them. This is all part of math talk.

6. Use cooperative learning and peer tutoring whenever possible so children can hear the math terms being used by other students.

7. Incorporate writing assignments in math so students can develop math vocabulary because they are utilizing those words. Having students write in a journal about how to solve an addition problem and writing key words on the board that they must use such as addends, plus, sum, regroup, ones column, and tens column, will give the students added experience with those words.

8. Use children's literature whenever possible in math class or even at home to provide an enriched environment for learning new words. Some possible books are already listed in a previous chapter. The librarians at the local library can offer suggestions of books that can be used for enhancing the learning process.

9. Teach students how to read their math textbooks. This can be an invaluable way to add the necessary vocabulary. Using reading in the content areas does include math instruction time.

10. Encourage students to use the glossary and the class dictionaries.
11. Maintain a word wall for math vocabulary.
12. Play games like Twenty Questions to make practicing math vocabulary fun.
13. Illustrate the meaning of math vocabulary and post these illustrations around the room.
14. Maintain flash cards of key words in math class and review them frequently. This is discussed in further detail later on in this chapter.
15. Have the students create a vocabulary section for their math binder. This can be of tremendous value and is discussed in further detail later on in this chapter.

What should be on that flash card? On one side, the students print the math term. On the other side, they either print the definition or give an example or even both. Perhaps they could even have a simple illustration of the concept on the card.

How often should these cards be reviewed with the children? The class should review these cards on a daily basis until the new words become a natural part of their math vocabulary. Then periodically they can review the flash cards. When the word bank grows, the students might review different words each day. The review should be done quickly. If not, then the math vocabulary has not been fully learned.

How else can these math words be reviewed? One of the ways those words could be reviewed is to place some of the definitions and/or examples face up on a table. As a child picks up one of the cards, he says the term that corresponds to the definition/ example. If he is correct, then he places that card aside. If he isn't, then he needs to return that card to the group. Next, he picks a different card and repeats the process. He can do this until all of the cards have been placed aside. Since the answer is always on the other side, the child can do this activity independently.

For a warm up in the beginning of math class, the teacher could write the vocabulary word on the board or overhead projector. Along with that word, two or three other words that are related to the vocabulary word should be written. The children would use those words in sentences to demonstrate how well they understood the math word. Next, the students share their sentences aloud with the class.

If there is a particular word a child has difficulty in remembering, the teacher could pin that card on his shirt. During the day, periodically someone asks him what word corresponds with the definition. Repetition helps.

The students should have a section in their math notebooks or binders for math vocabulary. As they learn new words or need to review math terms from previous years, the students can put these words in the vocabulary section. The students could draw pictures to illustrate the meaning of the math word as well as give examples and definitions.

When do students use the vocabulary section? During a daily math drill, the students could frequently use their vocabulary section to answer questions. Some of the assigned class work or homework assignments could be reviewing their vocabulary by having to answer a question about this section. The parents could sign a sheet stating they helped their children review their words, especially if the words are new and/or if any of the words are giving the students some difficulty. When the teacher quizzes the students on their vocabulary, they could refer to this section if needed. The teacher could also assign the students the task of creating a crossword puzzle for sharing. Whenever the teacher assigns an activity and someone forgets the meaning of a particular word, that student should refer to the vocabulary section before he/she is permitted to ask for assistance.

As teachers and parents work with children on math, they should all make sure they use math terminology. This should be done on a daily basis. The math terminology should become second nature.

- Math terminology should be used:
- As a new concept is introduced
- As the problems are discussed
- As the lessons are discussed
- As the students ask questions
- As the teachers and parents ask questions and the students give answers
- As teachers and parents help the students make connections with other math concepts
- As teachers and parents have the students explain orally how they solved the problems
- As the students write an explanation on how they solved the problems

However, if people's names are giving children difficulty, they should be allowed to substitute those names with ones they know. Quite often children spend a lot of time on sounding out unknown names and forget the gist of the problem. The class is not discussing a main character. Instead, the class is learning and reviewing math concepts.

"Knowledge has to be improved, challenged, and increased constantly, or it vanishes." Peter F. Drucker, American writer and management consultant.

Chapter 4

How Often Should Students Solve Word Problems in Math Class

Every day teachers and parents teach mathematics, they should have a word problem for students to solve. Yes, **everyday**. Solving word problems on a daily basis:

- Varies the work to keep it from being too humdrum
- Reinforces what is being taught
- Helps the children apply previously taught skills
- Immerses the children in the world of solving word problems until it becomes natural
- Helps students become determine to work until they find the solutions

Solving word problems everyday varies the work to keep it from being too humdrum and reinforces what is being taught. When children solve a series of addition problems over and over again, boredom often sets in. Although repetition is important to mastering a skill, teachers and parents must use a variety of activities to prevent students' disinterest in completing assignments. If they have students apply the new skill in solving related word problems, the skill becomes more meaningful, thereby they are increasing the probability of the students mastering the new concept.

Here is an example.

Mrs. Harris assigned her daughter, Caitlin, eight addition problems like the one below.

46

+ 8

This is addition with regrouping in the ones column, a skill that Caitlin is beginning to master, but still needs to practice. However, her mother realizes that if she doesn't vary the work, her daughter will lose interest. So she mixes word problems with some of the addition with regrouping. This way Caitlin can see why she needs to practice. The following is an example of what Mrs. Harris prepared for Caitlin.

1. 46   2. 54   3. 72   4. 35

  + 8   + 9   + 8   + 7

5. Phil has 28 coins in his collection. At the coin show, he bought 4 more. How many does he have now?

6. In her bedroom, Caitlin has 57 stuffed animals. Since she loves stuffed animals so much, her family and friends bought her some. They gave her a stuffed cat, dog, monkey, bird, and a mouse. How many does she have after her birthday?

7. The balloon man sold 39 balloons during the parade. At the carnival, he sold 8 more. In total, how many balloons did the balloon man sell?

8. Yesterday the elephants ate 25 bales of hay. So far today, they had eaten 7 bales of hay. Altogether, they ate how many bales of hay?

Often, Mrs. Harris will even use word problems when she first introduces a new skill to her children. Once again, she is varying the work along with showing the importance of the skill. Next week, she will have a word problem with this skill during drill time just to make sure that mastery has really set in.

Both teachers and parents need to be careful where they find those word problems. The typical elementary math textbook often has a pattern to their chapters. First the book gives an explanation and examples. Then there are number problems to do. Finally, there are word problems using that particular skill. They are necessary to give students practice in the concept being taught as well as the problem solving model being used, but they are very useful so long as they have been varied.

For example, a given chapter might give an explanation on how to add three digit numbers with regrouping once. Next, there are number problems to work on. Afterwards, there are word problems using the exact same skill. Quite often, the word problem only involves two numbers. Therefore, even if a child did not understand very many words in the word problem, the routine would be the same, and the child would know how to solve the problem. Having a routine is fine, but children need to be able to move on to different problems.

Many children tend to stop reading and analyzing the problem. Instead, they just take the two numbers and use whatever skill that they were working on which is completely the opposite of what the teachers want them to learn. Often the math texts in the primary grades give the operational signs for some word problems. So when these youngsters go to third grade, they are overwhelmed because the signs are no longer given.

Then too, children are linear thinkers in that they try to make the numbers match the problem in the exact order the numbers appeared in the word problem.

Here is an example:

Bobby had 35 baseball cards. He gave three to his cousin. How many does he have now?

There is no thinking here. It is obvious 35 is the first number and 3 is the next. If this problem came at the end of the basic subtraction chapter, then the student would know automatically to write 35–3 = 32.

But suppose the problem was written like this:

Bobby gave three of his baseball cards to his cousin. He started with 35. How many does he have now?

The students might give up too easily since the problem did not quite follow the step by step routine they had been using. That is why it is important to give the students word problems written in various ways. There is nothing wrong with having word problems with each new skill, but there must be some variation to the problems. Perhaps the teacher could have extra numbers and some of the problems might not have enough information for solving. The children could rewrite those problems so there was enough information and then exchange "their" revised problems with a partner.

When constructing a worksheet, the teacher should mix the skills. Using word problems with different skills that were previously taught could help prevent the lack of concentration and thinking. Sometimes the teacher might just want to discuss the problems at the end of the chapters.

Solving word problems everyday helps the children apply previously taught skills. Here is one way for the teacher to help the students maintain their skills. In order to reinforce math skills just taught, the teacher could assign students word problems that would have them apply those skills. Later on, students could solve word problems that would involve a mixture of math skills.

Suppose the teacher had taught addition and subtraction skills with two and three digit numbers in early fall. Then in the middle of winter, he could assign word problems that involve those same skills, but mix those problems with others using different skills.

For example:

1. Brian built a bookcase with three shelves. If he can fit 10 books, all of which are the same size, in the first shelf, what would the total number of books he could possibly fit in the whole bookcase if the remaining books are the same size as the ones on the first shelf?
2. This summer Marybeth bought 34 tiny stuffed animals for her bedroom. Yesterday, she gave seventeen of them to her friend. How many does she have now?
3. The art teacher was preparing for school. She bought 30 boxes of crayons. Each box had 24 crayons. Each box costs $.35. How much did she spend on those crayons?

The word problem involving subtraction with 2 digit numbers was placed in the middle of other problems. This way, the students are practicing the subtraction skill as well as other skills they have learned. This activity could have used a word problem that the students had already solved, but the numbers would be changed.

Solving word problems everyday immerses the children until it becomes natural. The more often children solve word problems, the more comfortable they are with the thinking processes used towards seeking the solutions. The children gain confidence in their achievements and feel good about mathematics. If children do word problems often enough, they become quite adept in applying the problem solving model. In this way, the model becomes a habit whenever they see the problems even when more advanced skills are involved.

Solving word problems everyday helps students become determined to work until they find the solutions. All teachers and parents want their students to become determined in searching for solutions to word problems. As the students mature and encounter more difficult word problems, that determination becomes more important. That determination helps students be more willing to face challenges in the different levels of mathematics such as algebra, geometry, and trigonometry.

"Solving problems is a practical art, like swimming, or skiing, or playing the piano: you can learn it only by imitation and practice . . . . if you wish to learn swimming you have to go in the water, and if you wish to become a problem solver you have to solve problems." George Polya

Chapter 5

Polya's 4-Step Problem Solving Model

When children face word problems, they are confronted with an overload of stimulation. Problems often require the students to do many things simultaneously. More complex problems or problems that need a different method for solving other than computation can cause math anxiety.

Teachers and parents can help students feel more comfortable with problem solving. How? Children can be empowered by their teachers and parents when they learn logical reasoning processes to analyze word problems. Children must be given an organized model to guide them with the dissecting of the problem. That model must be able to suit the students' needs since each group of students have a wide range of abilities, skill levels, and learning styles. Students must be given time to master the use of the model.

Teachers need to start with problems that are really exercises since the strategy is obvious. This is useful and lends to self confidence in math since the solutions are so similar. Students need these exercises to gain mastery of using the model as well as feeling good about their abilities to solve word problems.

However, math is more than obvious answers. Creatively seeking solutions is a major part of math. That can happen when the students feel confident and are ready.

The components of any problem solving model do not necessarily promise a solution. Simply they are to be used as a guide. After all, problem solving is a thinking process which has no set method. Encourage students to identify the difference between the recalling of information to provide an answer and the use of problem-solving strategies to provide a solution (Nitert, 1996).

In 1945, a mathematician named George Polya developed the four-step problem-solving model that many teachers and parents use today in instructing children how to solve word problems. **"To have a problem means to search consciously for some action appropriate to attain some clearly conceived but not immediately attainable aim. To solve a problem means to find such an action"** (George Polya).

In the back of the book, a copy of the Polya's Problem Solving Model is included so teachers and parents may make two copies for each student. One copy would be for their math binder, while the other copy would be for home use. The problem solving model could also be placed on posters. The art teacher could have a contest to see which student can create the best character(s) that would add appeal to the problem solving model. The problem solving model in the appendix also includes the questions below each part to guide the students.

The Four-Step Problem Solving Model-The Simplified Version

Understand the problem

Develop a plan to solve the problem

Carry out the plan

Look back

The next few pages will explain each step in detail as well as offer some suggestions for implementing. Here is Step 1.

1. Understanding the problem

- Read the problem.
- Do you understand the problem?
- Reread the problem if you don't understand it.
- Can you rephrase the problem in a statement?
- Highlight key words.
- What are you trying to solve or find out?
- What are the unknowns?
- Which information did you find in the problem?
- Which information is missing?
- Which information is not needed?

The questions are guidelines to help students understand what the problem is asking. The first step is obvious since students have to read the problem. However, students should become use to asking themselves, "Do I understand this problem?" If they don't, then they should reread the problem.

For the first reading of the word problem, the students should be allowed to substitute unknown words with a nonsense word so they can complete their reading. **Why?** It is important for the students to complete their first reading of the problem without a lot of interruptions. Afterwards, they can either look up the word in the dictionary or use their own vocabulary dictionary for assistance.

Can the students locate the question to be solved? Sometimes students do not even know what the problem is asking them to do. If they do not know what the question is, then how can they solve the problem? The students might need to practice pinpointing what the problem is asking them to do.

Can they rephrase the problem in a statement? This is important since it will let teachers and parents know whether or not the students truly understand the problem. If there are names in the problem that students are not use to seeing, they should substitute them with names they know.

When teachers introduce problem solving to students, they should have them do the following activity. Students have to be able to locate the question being solved. Sometimes that is not as easy as it sounds. Depending upon the grade level and ability of the students, the teachers may have to modify the activity or just use one type of word problem at a time until the students are comfortable with locating the question. The activity is located in the Appendix in larger font.

The four examples could be placed on a transparency or on chart paper so the whole class can see what is being discussed. After they have discussed each example, then they can look at a variety of word problems found in both the math text and reproducible worksheets.

This can be accomplished in a variety of ways. For the first way, divide the class into groups of 4 and assign each group some problems for finding the questions. The groups will have chart paper and marker to record their ideas. Then someone from each group will share their work.

For the second way, divide the class into student pairs. Assign each pair of students a few problems to search for the questions. Each pair could either be given chart paper and a marker or a transparency and pen to record their ideas. One member of each pair will share their ideas with the class.

Finding the Question

When you have word problems to solve, the first step is to decide what the problem is asking you to do. Find the question, but you must use your own words.

1. Some word problems only have one sentence.
    How much money do you owe when you buy three candy bars at $.50 each?

    The question asks . . . How much did you spend on the three candy bars?

2. Some word problems have two sentences. One sentence has the information you need to solve the problem. The other one has the question.

Tomas bought a shirt for $12.85 at The Clothing Mart and then he bought a shirt for $14.97 at The Shirt Mart. How much more did the shirt from The Shirt Mart cost than the shirt from The Clothing Mart?

The question asks . . . How much more did one shirt cost than the other?

3. There are word problems that have two sentences where each one has important information for solving the problem.

The Game Shop sells computer games for $15.75 each. If Allen has a $50 gift certificate, how many games can he buy?

The question asks . . . How many games can he buy?

4. The question sometimes might not have a question mark.

At the Game Shop, the computer games normally sell for $15.75 each, but today they are 20% off. Find out how much each game costs with the sale.

The question asks . . . Find out the new price with the sale.

For the next activity, students will be practicing rephrasing the question in statement form. If the problems are too difficult for any of the students, the teacher could either use lower numbers or rewrite the problems so they only deal with the skill level students have reached.

Once again, after modeling how to rephrase the questions into statement form, the teacher assign the students the task of doing the same with a worksheet or a page from their math text. They could work in groups of 4 or in pairs. Each group or pair writes their statements on chart paper or transparency so they can share their work with the class. The students can ask questions for the group or pair that is sharing to help clarify any areas of confusion.

If parents are home schooling their children, this activity can still be used. The parents model how to rephrase the questions in statement form. They and their children could take turns in rephrasing the questions. This activity is also located in the Appendix.

Rephrasing the Question in Statement Form.

Read each problem. Find the question. Then rephrase the question in statement form. Leave a blank in the statement for the answer.

1. Bria's birthday was today and she wanted to celebrate it with her classmates in school. She decided to bring 96 Willy Wonka candy bars to give to her 24 classmates. How many candy bars will each classmate receive if Bria distributes them equally?

2. Terrence rode on the subway in the city quite frequently to go to various places. He rode on the Yellow Line 72 times last year. During that same year, he rode the Red Line 48 times more than he did the Yellow Line. How many times did Terrance ride on the Red Line last year?

3. The train from Stansfield to Eldersville makes 789 stops along the route. The same train continues from Eldersville to Miden Heights with 43 stops. How many stops altogether does this train make?

4. Mr. Bee baked cinnamon cookies for the school's bake sale. He decided to put 3 cookies in each bag. If he had 12 bags, how many cinnamon cookies did he bake for the bake sale?

5. Last year, Mr. Bee baked 48 cinnamon cookies for the school's bake sale. How many more cookies did he bake last year than he did this year?

Highlighting key words

If consumable workbooks or worksheets are being used, then teachers should allow students to highlight key words and numbers in the problem. The class should take the time to discuss their choices of key words. Modeling how to find the key words is important if the students are doing this type of activity for the first time or if students are having difficulty with locating key words.

Key words for problems requiring equations are usually easy to find. However, teachers need to keep in mind that sometimes these problems might not have the obvious keys words. Therefore, students need plenty of practice with problems that do not contain those key words.

As the students work on word problems dealing with addition, they should look for key words that denote addition. The whole class should keep a chart of these words for everyone to see as they work on word problems. Whenever someone finds a new key word, that student proves this new key word is for addition. Then the word is added to the class list. The students could also keep a list for their own math binders so they can refer to the list during class work, homework, or for summer review. This process should be repeated for subtraction, multiplication, and division.

The following pages show possible key words for all 4 operations. Depending upon the age and skill level of the students, the teacher might not want to show all of the key words at one time. Using the discovery method during the year might be more appropriate for the children, but the list could be used to guide the teacher. If the teacher thinks the students are ready for some of the more difficult key words but the class has not found them, then the teacher could rewrite some problems using those very words.

Since some of the words can be used for more than one operation teachers and parents need to be careful in helping students make that distinction. For example, the word total can be used for both addition and multiplication. Therefore, teachers and parents need to help students see that using key words can be helpful as well as confusing. The following pages are also located in the Appendix.

Key Words for the Four Operations

If you are working on word problems that work well with equations or using addition, subtraction, multiplication, and division, identifying key words or phrases can help. However, keep in mind that not every problem will contain these words.

Addition	Subtraction
How many	How much more
Altogether	Which is more
Combine	By how much
Total	Difference
Sum	Remove
How much	Decreased by
Increased by	Minus
Together	Less
Added to	Less than
Both	Fewer than
In all	How many more
Additional	Left
Another	Remain
Raise	Take away
Perimeter	Dropped, Lost, Fell

Words ending in er such as heavier, taller, smaller, lighter, faster, slower, farther, higher, lower . . . usually signify subtraction

Multiplication	Division
Product	Share
Total	Distribute
Area	Quotient
Times	Average
Multiplied	Equally
Increased by	In each
Decreased by	Per
Percent	Separate . . . equally
Factor	Ratio
Every	Percent
At this rate	Split
Each	Equal pieces
Doubled, Tripled, or Quadrupled	Cut
As much	

Missing information or too much information

Quite often word problems contain more information than is needed to find the solution. Sometimes word problems might be missing key information. **Given information** refers to all of the information that a problem contains. **Necessary information** refers only to the numbers and labels vital to finding a solution that makes sense to the question. **Extra information** refers to the information in a given problem that is not vital to finding a solution that makes sense to the question.

Practice and think aloud are needed in order to help students locate only the information that is needed to solve the problem. Quite often teachers and parents might need to rewrite word problems to make sure those problems contain extra information. By doing this, students will have ample practice in locating **necessary information** and **extra information**.

Pass out a worksheet that has several word problems. Some of them are ready to be solved as they are, while others contain extra information. Assign each group of 4 students some problems to study carefully. Ask them to find the **necessary information** and the **extra information**. Below each problem have them write the necessary information on the left while they write the extra information on the right. Emphasize they are not to solve these problems. Then have a class discussion about these problems. Allow the students to make corrections to what they found after the class has discussed each question.

Another way to do this activity is to divide the class into groups of 4 again. Give each group 2 problems to modify. For one word problem they must omit some key information, while for the other problem they must add some extra information. Make sure the students understand that the extra information should still be related to the theme of the problem, just not key to the solution.

For example,

1. Mr. Jackson's students will walk to the picnic area with adult chaperones. He has 25 students and 5 adults. He assigned one of the parents to help him carry the drinks while two other parents carried the treats. How many groups of students will be walking to the picnic area?
2. For the class picnic, Mr. Jackson bought juice boxes that come 4 to a package, five large bags of pretzels, and five boxes of treats that come 5 to a box. If each person drinks one juice box, how many packages of juice boxes will Mr. Jackson need to buy so everyone on the picnic will have something to drink?

For problem #1, the students could omit how many students there were or they could omit the total number of parents on the trip. For the same problem, they could add that one of the students had brought his iPod along. He was so busy listening to his music that he was almost left behind. For problem #2, the fact that the juice boxes came 4 to a package could be left out.

After giving the groups sufficient time to complete the assignment, then have them share how they modified the problems. They could write the new problems on chart paper so they could show the rest of the class, or they could exchange papers with another group so each group can solve the problems.

Can other students still solve any of the questions? Why or why not? This could lead into a nice discussion on how the modifications affected their ability to solve some of the problems yet at the same time they had the opportunity to see what each group did.

Let's look at Step 2 of Polya's problem solving model.

2. Develop a plan to solve the problem

Below are some of the strategies that are quite useful in solving problems.

- Draw a picture
- Write an equation
- Use guess and check
- Look for a pattern
- Examine related problems to see if the same strategy can be used or applied
- Examine a simpler case of the problem for further understanding
- Make a table
- Make a diagram
- Work backwards
- Identify a subgoal-Some problems may have more than one step
- Make an organized list
- Use logic

In developing the plan, it is important to note that not all word problems lend themselves to equations. Many do, but also many do not. Some word problems might involve more than one strategy, while others can be solved in more than one way. The key is to help the students identify the difference. In other words, the students practice identifying when to use guess and test, patterns, subgoals, an organized list, table, and so on.

There are many books on the market that propose to help students solve word problems, but they do not always cover all of the strategies. This does not mean they are not helpful, just limited in scope since some of the strategies involving representations, such as drawing a picture, drawing a diagram, creating a chart or table, and making an organized list are not included in the books.

Each strategy listed on the previous page has a main problem for students to work on together when the teacher first introduces that particular strategy. A copy of all of the problems is located in the Appendix. However, the problems in the Appendix do not show the answer key. For each strategy some situations are listed when that particular strategy might be most useful. Posters or small copies of these situations could be created for students to use as references.

Draw a Picture

Sometimes the students need to draw a picture to help them figure how to solve the problem especially if any of those students are visual learners. The picture does not have to be realistic or in detail. Rather a simple figure such as a rectangle could be used, one for each book in the problem below. Students could even use graph paper to help them out. Each square on the graph could represent a book.

For example,

The school library held a book sale. Carla bought 3 books. Then her mother came in to the sale and bought Carla 6 books. How many books does she have now?

Teachers and parents can instruct children to use Draw a Picture strategy by sharing some key points to look out for such as:

- A visual representation would be most helpful in solving the problem.
- The student is a visual learner.
- Geometric shapes or measurements are sometimes used in the problem.

Write the Equation

For many of the word problems children will probably need to use equations. As the students read the problems, they need to look for clue words and highlight them. Referring to the list under Understanding the Problem or in the Appendix for clue words can be most helpful. Then the students look for the numerical information that would be important to solving the problems.

For example,

Shawn and Brea bought lunch at the card show. Brea spent $9.75 on a tuna sandwich and a soda. Shawn spent $12.40 on a hamburger, fries, and a soda. How much less did Brea spend on lunch than Shawn?

The clue word is less which means to subtract since the problem is comparing Shawn's and Brea's lunch. $12.40–$9.75 = $2.65

Teachers and parents can instruct children to use Write the Equation strategy by sharing some key points to look out for such as:

- The problem has clues guiding the students to use addition, subtraction, multiplication, or/and division
- Nothing else will solve the problem.
- The answers make sense.

Use Guess and Test

In guess and test, the students need to make an educated guess for solving the problem. Then they test their possible solution. If that attempt does not work, then they need to try another idea. These attempts are called trials. In order to make sure they are not using the same solutions over and over or haphazardly looking for ideas, the students should record each solution. The recording of each trial also gives them the opportunity to see how they can modify or totally change their method of solving the problem.

For example,

Activity	Costs
Miniature Golf	$3.50
Skating	$2.50
Go-Kart Rides	$2.75
Skate Boarding	$3.25
Ping-Pong	$2.25

Tomas decided to go to Fun World where there are various activities that children of all ages can do. He picked two of the activities from a chart of five. He paid with a ten dollar bill. He received $4 as his change. Which two activities did he do? Was that the only answer to this problem? Show your work.

In the above problem, students need to be organized in looking for combinations that will end up giving $4 as change from $10. This is a great problem for the teacher to model how to pick two activities at a time, record what was picked, how much the two cost together, and how much change was received from $10. This particular problem involves more than one possible answer.

Since the problem gave the amount of change of $4, students need to subtract 4 from 10 to see how much two of the activities need to add up to. Teachers should ask the students what should be done first before they start looking for combinations of two activities. Students could discuss this in a group and the teacher could use Numbered Heads Together to pick one person from each group to share their answers. If none of the groups figured that they need to pick two activities that equaled $6, then the teacher needs to guide the class through that part of the problem with some questions.

Organizing the combinations is important. Being organized helps the problem solver make an educated guess. There are other ways to organize the combinations. Teachers need to choose one way that will be suitable for their students. Here is one way to do this:

Use abbreviations for each activity.

MG-Miniature golf S-Skating GK-Go-Kart Rides SK-Skateboarding P—Ping-Pong

MG + S = $6 S + GK = $5.25 GK + SK = $6 SK + P = $5.50

MG + GK = $6.25 S + SK = $5.75 GK + P = $5

MG + SK = $6.75 S + P = $4.75

MG + P = $5.75

After the organized list has been completed, the students look for the combinations that fit the problem. In this case, there are two answers.

Miniature golf and skating   Go-kart racing and skateboarding

After reviewing this problem, teachers can see what students can do with a similar problem. The teachers could also add two other activities to the chart. The students could discuss with a partner or in small groups what they would need to do in order to solve the problem with the two extra activities.

Teachers and parents can instruct children to use Guess and Test strategy by sharing some key points to look out for such as:

- The potential answers being investigated are limited.
- Use an organized approach for investigating each possibility.
- Students make an educated guess by looking at clues found in the problem as well as their organized list.

Look for a Pattern

Patterns are found everywhere. Developing skills in looking for patterns can be useful not only in everyday life, but also in language arts, mathematics, science, history, music, art, and physical education. For younger students, patterns are found in counting, learning the alphabet, stringing beads, and creating a design using pattern blocks. As the students grow older, they are able to study the patterns and determine what is next. They soon learn how to discover the rule that governs what is next to a particular arrangement.

Often, students need to construct a chart or table to look over the items or numbers in the pattern. By discovering the relationships of the numbers or items that help form the pattern, they can find the rule. Then this rule can help them predict what is next in the pattern. They can even predict the rest of the pattern before they extend it.

For example,

Nancy's family room floor is done in square tiles. She was noticing how the small squares can form larger squares. As Nancy studied these different size squares she discovered there were patterns in the perimeters and areas of those squares. What patterns in the squares' perimeters and areas do you think she might have found?

Can Nancy use those patterns to predict what the perimeters and areas of even larger squares would be?

By using graph paper, preferably with squares of 1 cm size, the students draw squares of different sizes. This could be done individually, in pairs, or in small groups depending upon the confidence and skill level of the class.

For sharing the various squares each group has found, the students could draw one of their solutions on a transparency of the graph paper. The teacher can walk around the room to find examples of different answers. When a different square has been located, the teacher needs to call on someone from the group to share the square on the transparency. Next, the students discuss what they notice about the different squares. Are the squares similar? Congruent? Do they have the same area? Do they have the same perimeter? This would be a great time to discuss the above terms in case any of the students do not know or recognize them. Afterwards the students need to discuss how the sharing helped them discover the pattern.

By using questions, the teachers guide them to the idea of an organized list. Patterns and organized lists go together. Have them discuss what that organized might look like. Below is one possibility.

Square	Perimeter	Area
1	4	1
2	8	4
3	12	9
4	16	16
5	20	25
6	24	36
7		
8		

Here are some possible questions to ask students.

- What is happening with the numbers on the list as they read across?
- Is there a relationship between the square label numbers and the perimeters?
- Is there a relationship between the square label numbers and the areas?
- Look down the perimeter column from top to bottom. Do you notice anything?
- Look down the area column from top to bottom. Do you notice anything here?
- How are the various rows and columns related?

Predict the perimeters and areas for the next few squares without the graph paper. Can you use the patterns to form your predictions?

After the students have discussed the above questions, they should write an analysis of their findings. They need to include in their analysis the answers to the original problem. For an extension of this particular problem, the students do the same problem, but this time there are dots on each corner of each square within the larger squares. So for square 1 there will be 4 dots. For square 2, there will be four small squares and each one will have dots on the corners for a total of 9. For the square 3, there will be 12 dots. For another extension, have the students create rectangles. The length and width would increase by one each time. The possibilities are endless for this.

Teachers and parents can instruct children to use Look for a Pattern strategy by sharing some key points to look out for such as:

- Problem gives a list of data and numbers.
- The problem contains a series of numbers or a series of related figures.
- Need to predict or generalize.
- Listing certain situations helps the students with complex problems.
- The information can be presented an organized table or list.

Making a Table

For example,

Mr. Danver has a landscaping business called The Green Thumb. His son, Rudy, was collecting data on how many jobs the business had each month from March to September.

Rudy's data was: March-20; April-55; May-70; June-65; July-55; August-35; September-70

Construct a table for Rudy's data collection. Next, use the information to construct a bar graph. After carefully studying both the table and the graph, think about why each month had a certain number of jobs. Did March have the fewest because not everyone was ready for planting? At first, there was plenty of rain, but one month there was a drought. Why do you think there were plenty of jobs for May and June?

Now write an analysis of the findings. In that analysis figure out which month there was a drought, which month people wanted their gardens prepared for the winter, and which months were the busiest. Explain your answers in detail. Also, in the analysis, predict what the table and bar graph might look like for next year and explain why you think that.

Example of what the table might look like.

The Green Thumb Business

Month	Jobs
March	20
April	55
May	70
June	65
July	55
August	35
September	70

Since this problem deals with a gardening business the teacher might want to see how much students know about gardening before they attempt to solve the problem. Do they know the best months for planting? Which month might people mulch and what is mulching? When can people start gardening? Depending upon the area of the country, people, who want a garden, generally need to wait until the last frost has hit. Otherwise, they will have to plant all over again. By accessing the prior knowledge of the students, the teachers are helping the students share what they already know. Teachers are also connecting a word problem with the real world which is important to students' learning.

Teachers and parents can instruct children to use Make a Table strategy by sharing some key points to look out for such as:

- Information can easily be organized.
- Information was from a data collection.
- Graphing can be the product of the information organizing.

Work Backward

Tommy, Donnie, and Bonnie are three of Dr. Samson's children. Tommy is 3 years older than Donnie. Bonnie is 15 years old which is 5 years older than Tommy. How old is Donnie?

Which clue is obvious? Yes, Bonnie is 15 years old. That is our starting point. Which clue hints at Tommy's age? Well, the problem states that Bonnie is 5 years older than Tommy. So we need to solve Tommy's age by subtracting 5 from 15. Tommy is 10 years old. The first clue was the vaguest, but since we now know how old Tommy is, we can use that clue. The problem stated that Tommy is 3 years older than Donnie. We need to solve Donnie's age by subtracting. Donnie is 7 years old.

By locating the facts the children know and moving backwards, they can solve this problem. Once the children have done this particular problem, the teachers could erase the numbers and fill in others that will work here. Then assign the problem by having the students work in pairs or in groups to solve the problem. Have them discuss what was easy and what was difficult about this type of problem. Did they see how the beginning of the problem was complex and not clear, but the ending was more simplified and the result was clear?

Working backwards is similar to solving logic problems that use clues and a grid. However, the logic problems are usually more involved. Just like the working backward problem, the logic generally has a clue that is pretty obvious and must be used to solve some of the others. This particular strategy would be a good one to use just before solving logic problems using those grids.

Teachers and parents can instruct children to use Work Backward strategy by sharing some key points to look out for such as:

- The end result is clear, but the first part is not.
- The ending of the problem is simple.
- The beginning is intricate.
- The word problem has a sequence of actions which can be switched around.

Identify a Subgoal-Some problems may have more than one step.

For example,

Maria loves shopping. She loves to shop so much that she drives to the Senator Mall once a week. Two weeks ago, Maria visited seven stores, but only made purchases at two.

First, Maria went to Music City, a place that specializes in all items of music. She browsed for 2 hours before making a decision on what to buy. At the checkout counter, she had 3 CDs that were priced at $10.99 each and 1 second hand CD priced at $5.95. During this time, she gave the sales associate 2 twenty dollar bills.

What was Maria's change?

In order to find a solution, students will have to realize that this is a multi-step problem. They need to look for the subgoals. While doing this, they also need to discuss what subgoals are and how many word problems have them.

Teachers can help students identify what needs to be done first. Role play and drawings can help here. The main thing is for students to see that to find out Maria's change, the first step is to find the total cost of the purchases. Since the purchases involve different items, that could mean another step.

The 3 CDs cost $10.99 each. What should students do to find the total cost of the 3 CDs? The students could either add $10.99 three times or multiply $10.99 by 3. What needs to be done next? How should the student solve the next part of this problem? Since they are finding how much change is left, what algorithm should be used? Subtraction of course. If the high numbers confused some of the students, the teacher could substitute smaller numbers for the prices or omit the $.99 and $.95.

The teacher could give the students a worksheet containing a few word problems with subgoals. Either by themselves, or in groups, teachers should have the students locate the subgoals in each problem by underlining each subgoal with a different colored pencil. Teachers should not have their students solve the problems yet, but rather discuss the subgoals in each problem. Each group could be responsible for a different problem and have their work on a transparency so they could show their answers on the overhead. After the students discussed the answers, then the teacher could have the students solve the problems on their own.

Perhaps the teacher could permit the students to choose a certain number of problems to do. For example, suppose there were 10 problems. Students could do at least four of those problems, but they choose which ones to solve. Children like choices. The act of choosing makes them feel that they are in charge of their work.

Teachers and parents can instruct children to use Identify a Subgoal strategy by sharing some key points to look out for such as:

•A problem has more than one part to solve.
•The problem's statement is long and contains more than one step.
•There is a simpler step further in the problem that would be helpful to solve first.
•Solving one part of the problem helps solving another part of the problem.

Examine a Simpler Case of the Problem for Further Understanding

The students should refer to the problem solving journal to find other problems dealing with finding change. As a matter of fact, the student should be referring to this journal daily for reviewing the solutions for the previous word problems. The reviews could be done per teachers' instructions. Perhaps the teachers want them to review any problems dealing with patterns. Then they could review those problems. Perhaps the students could be given the direction of finding a problem similar, but simpler to the one that was just placed in front of them to solve. As the students mature, they should divide their journal in sections. Each section could be for a type of strategy that was used to solve a problem.

Here's the second part of Maria's day at the mall.

Maria went to Girls' Boutique where she tried on five blouses, three skirts, and eight necklaces. After some careful thinking, she decided on three blouses which cost $21.99,

$18.50, and $26.99. She also bought two skirts which cost $35.99 each. How much money did she spend at this store?

Shopping made Maria hungry so she stopped at the Blue Jay Inn where she met her friend, Holly. After the two of them read the menu posted outside the restaurant, they decided to go in.

Maria ordered a salad at $5.75, a deluxe cheeseburger at $8.99, and an ice tea for $1.50. Holly picked the crab cake sandwich for $9.50, fries at $1.50, and a soda for $2.50. Who spent more for their lunch and by how much?

The students should think about how this problem is similar to the simpler problem they had located in their journals. Then they need to think about how it is different. To assist them with the task of comparing and contrasting the two problems, the students could even complete a Venn diagram! Afterwards the students could discuss the similarities and differences.

Teachers and parents can instruct children to use Examine a Simpler Case strategy by sharing some key points to look out for such as:

- Detailed and difficult calculations are part of the problem.
- Very large or very small numbers are contained in the problem.
- The sum of a series of numbers needs to be computed.

Make an Organized List

When there is need to make an organized list, the problem solvers are trying to see how many outcomes they can find to the same problem. The list needs to be organized so they do not duplicate any answers. Whenever teachers have students make an organized list, they should keep in mind that these lists can take different forms. A tree list can be used and is simple to organize so teachers might want to start the students with the tree list.

For example,

Mrs. Jackson bought some pants and shirts for her son, Jacob. She bought 4 pants-black, brown, blue, and tan. She also purchased 5 shirts-white, yellow, red, purple, and light blue.

How many different outfits can Jacob make with those 4 pants and 5 shirts?

What are the different outfits?

Teachers should model for their students how to make the tree list starting with one of the pants colors. Since there are 4 pant colors as opposed to 5 shirts colors, then start with the pants. This way, students will need to construct fewer tree lists. For the first try at constructing the tree list, teachers might want to instruct the students to write out the whole word for each color. After doing one, discuss what it means. How many outfits can Jacob create with black pants and five different shirts? Predict how many outfits Jacob will be able to create with brown pants. How do you know? Then have the students finish the tree list on their own. Here is one example of a tree list.

Black   —white

          —yellow

          —red

          —purple

          —light blue

Teachers and parents can instruct children to use Make an Organized List strategy by sharing some key points to look out for such as:

- Facts and figures are easily prepared and shared.
- Data is easily generated.
- Recording the outcomes found by using *Guess and Test*.
- The phrase, "In how many ways", is used in the problem.
- A set of numbers produced by a rule or formula.

Draw a Diagram

One type of diagram is the Venn diagram, which was created by John Venn, a lecturer from the 1800s and specialized in logic. Venn diagrams are usually two intersecting circles. The section shared by both circles represents the ways the concepts are similar or what they share. For a concept that does not fit in any part of the two circles, a separate, but small circle is used.

To prepare the students for this activity, teachers can conduct a survey of their students. Here is one example on a survey that teachers can use. First write the number of students in the class on the board so all of the students can see it. Next, ask the students how many love both sports and watching TV. Then ask how many students love sports only. Afterwards, ask how many students love to watch TV only. Finally, ask how many students love neither activity. Construct the Venn diagram, label the two circles, draw the small circle on the outside of the diagram, and fill in the numbers. This is good practice for working with subsets. This activity also gives the students the opportunity to create their own surveys and even visit other classrooms to conduct the surveys.

Here is an example of a problem using the Venn diagram. Teachers need to keep in mind that this type of problem is a logic problem that uses a Venn diagram.

In a classroom of 45 students, 38 said they loved art and 27 said they loved music. Twenty-two students said that they loved both subjects. How many students in the classroom do not like either subject?

Draw two intersecting circles. For the one on the left, print I love art on top. For the one on the right, print I love music on top. In the cross section write 22. Why? The problem stated that 22 students loved both subjects. Next to the Venn diagram, put a smaller circle with a question mark inside. This smaller circle is for the number of students who like neither of those two subjects.

So what should be placed in the I love music circle? 38? No. Remember that the number 38 represents all of the students who love music. That means 22 students who love both subjects is part of that 38. For this problem, subtract 22 from 38 to see how many students only like music. For this section, use the number, 16.

For the I love art section, follow the same procedure. The problem stated that 27 loved art, but remember that 22 of the students loves both subjects. So again, subtract. 27—22 = 5   Five students love only art.

Let's refer to the problem again. It stated that there were 45 students. 16 loved music, and 5 loved art. We need to find out how many students liked neither subject. Add 16, 22, and 5 to get the number of students who loved those one or both of those subjects. That means 43 students loved art, music, or both. Subtract 43 from 45 to find that 2 students did not love either subject.

Here is an example of the Venn Diagram.

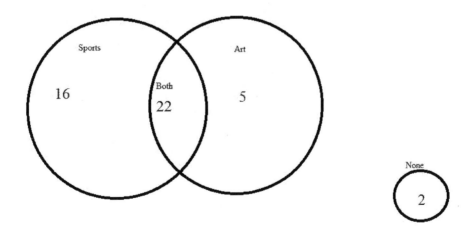

(The problem is in the Appendix, but without the Venn Diagram. Students can draw their own.)

There are several types of diagrams that can be used for problem solving. Teachers could even incorporate simple floor plans to have students work on perimeter and area. A diagram might even be a map where the students have to solve for distance traveled.

The activity of factoring numbers to the prime level lends itself to the diagram strategy. The possibilities are endless, but the teachers need to guide the children to using the ones they have been taught.

Teachers and parents can instruct children to use Draw a Diagram strategy by sharing some key points to look out for such as:

- The problem involves sets, prime factorization, ratios, probabilities, or possible answers.
- A diagram is more efficient than a picture.
- Looking for relationships of numbers
- Factor trees, tree lists, and connecting circles are just a few examples of possible diagrams.

Use Logic

For example,

There are five people in the Everhart family. They are Russell, Jean, John, Paul, and Mary. Their ages are 12, 20, 21, 39, and 45. Russell is the oldest member, while Jean is the youngest member of this family. John is 8 years older than Jean. Paul is not 45. How old is Mary? Construct a chart to help you sort through the clues.

	12	20	21	39	45
Russell	X	X	X	X	Yes
Jean					
John					
Paul					
Mary					

Teachers need to walk the children through the logic puzzle. Step by step, teachers put in the yes as they help the students sort through the clues. Before going on to the next clue, the teacher demonstrates how to place the X where it can no longer be a yes. The first clue states that Russell is the oldest member. So the students put a yes across the chart from Russell's name for 45. Then they place an X for each member of the family below the first yes. Now they place an x across the row with Russell's name. Before the teacher and students go any further, they can already see how that one clue narrows down what to choose for Everhart family and ages.

For the next clue, Jean is the youngest member. Since 12 is the lowest number, that is Jean's age. So the students need to place a yes beside Jean's name under the 12 column. Then they go down that column and place Xs for the rest of the family. Also, they need to move across Jean's row and place an X for the rest of the ages. When they are finished with this puzzle, the students will learn that Mary is 39.

	12	20	21	39	45
Russell	X	X	X	X	Yes
Jean	Yes	X	X	X	X
John	X	Yes	X	X	X
Paul	X	X	Yes	X	X
Mary	X	X	X	Yes	X

Teachers can use ages from one of the student's families to create a similar problem or work on an original one. See if the students can do the second one on their own. If there are students with reading difficulties, then perhaps they could work in pairs or in some groups.

Teachers and parents can instruct children to use the Use Logic strategy by sharing some key points to look out for such as:

- Several clues are given.
- Sometimes the starting point is not always easy to find
- Sometimes there is no starting point
- Reasoning is needed to complete the problem
- Can use what you know to draw conclusions about what you don't know

For each of the strategies, the teachers or parents can create a chart on what to look for in the word problem. The students could have a copy of this chart in their problem solving journal for future use. The students need the opportunity to determine which strategy to use; however, it might be prudent for the children to experience only a few different strategies at a time. In the problem solving journal, an example of each type of word problem could be included.

Carry out the Plan

- Use one or more of the strategies from Step 2
- Decide on what tools you will need to carry out your plan
- Check each step of the plan as you work.
- Keep an accurate record of your work.

In step 3 of the problem solving model, it is essential to have the students note that they are responsible for keeping an accurate record of their work. Discussing what their work should look like is important because this gives the teacher the opportunity to check their work and for them to check their own progress. The students could brainstorm which characteristics their work should have. Perhaps they could come up with a list like the one below. This list could even be used as a rubric for students grading the neatness and organization of their work. This checklist is in the Appendix for the convenience of the teachers and parents. This checklist could be copied and placed in the students' math binders as a reference.

In order for me to check my work and make sure it is accurate, I need to do the following:

- Write down the type of strategy that I am using.
- Make sure my work is neat.
- Be organized.
- If I must erase a part, then I must do it carefully.
- Leave spaces behind each portion of a problem.
- Leave spaces behind each problem so they don't run into each other as I recheck my work.
- List tools that I used other than a pencil and paper.
- Ask myself, "When I look over my work, will I be able to understand my own work?"
- Ask myself, "When my teacher or parent look over my work, will they be able to understand my work so they can help me and grade my work?"

Looking Back

- Check the results
- Does your answer make sense?
- Is your answer reasonable?
- Rework your problem if necessary or use another strategy

For step 4, students need to check over the results. For example, if they subtracted, then they should make sure they placed the correct number on top and add to check the answer. If they divided, they should make sure they placed the right number inside the radical sign, and then check their work by multiplying.

Teachers and parents need to emphasize that students should always ask themselves if their answers seem reasonable and make sense. To practice doing this, the teachers and parents could give them some word problems that have been solved. In groups, students check each part of the work and check for reasonable answers. Again, the groups share their findings.

Another way to practice is to keep a record of wrong answers from students' work. If they had just completed a worksheet on word problems that dealt with addition and subtraction, then the teachers and parents could share some of the unreasonable answers with the whole class. However they never reveal the students' names. Also they take the time to emphasize that the mistakes are not up for ridicule, but for examples on looking for reasonable answers, or perhaps they could tell the students that these answers came from previous years.

If the worksheet involved 10 problems, see if anyone missed the first problem. If so and the answer stemmed from giving an unreasonable answer, then that the first problem could be shown to the class for a discussion how the work led to the wrong solution. The same could be done for each problem, but one. One problem could have the correct answer to see if the students can spot the problem solved correctly.

While conducting this type of lesson, teachers should exercise caution to ensure they never take more than one wrong answer from the same student. It is important for them to refrain from being judgmental. Remember that what is obvious to an adult is not always obvious to a child. Also remember that quite often math anxiety is caused by the adult even though that adult never meant to do so.

The following pages show some word problems with wrong answers. Some of the wrong answers may be due to inaccurate estimating, choosing the wrong operation, making a careless mistake on the algorithm, not seeing the clue words, not having enough information, or using the extra information. Word problems from the students' text could also be used to make sure the problems are on their level. This worksheet is also located in the Appendix.

Is the Answer Reasonable?

1. Susie eats five cookies a day. How many cookies would she eat in a week?

    5 x 7 = 30 cookies

2. There are 596 students in the choir. The band has 237 fewer students than the choir. How many students are in the band?

    596

    +237

    833 students

3. David spent $96.73 on a pack of hockey cards at the card show. His dad spent $61.58 on a pack of soccer cards. How much did David and his dad spend altogether?

    $96.73 + $61.58 = $1,583. 10

4. Atticus has $90 from washing windows. He bought basketball shoes that cost $76.95 and a pair of socks that cost $7.96. How much money does he have left?

    $76.95 $90.00

    + 7.96   – 84.91

    $84.91 $ 5.09

5. There were 41 students playing soccer during recess. Eighteen were girls. How many were boys?

    18–41 = 37 boys

6. There were three teams playing during recess. The Red Team scored 18 points. The Blue team scored 5 more points than the Red Team. The Blue Team scored how many points?

    3 + 18 + 5 = 26 points

7. The library lent 8,545 books in the first marking period. In the second marking period, it lent over 6,000 books. How many more books did they lend in the first marking period than the second marking period?

6,000

−8,545

2,455 more books

8. There are 165 people waiting to ride on a roller coaster. If only 5 people can ride on the roller coaster at a time, how many rides does the roller coaster have to complete in order for each person waiting to get a ride?

165 / 5 = 31 rides

9. Ramona paid $58.86 for 6 pounds of shrimp for a party. How much does the shrimp cost per pound?

$58.86

x 6

$353.16

10. The zookeeper uses fresh hay each day in the elephants' stalls. He uses 5 bales of hay for each elephant stall. If there are 20 stalls, how many bales of hay does he need for one day? How many bales of hay does he need for 1 week?

5 x 20 = 100 bales of hay for one day 1 x 100 = 100 bales of hay for the week

Children should have access to a problem solving model to help them stay focus on what they need to do in order to solve the problem. In the Appendix, there is a copy of a checklist that will guide students on checking their work for accuracy and making sense. This checklist could be placed in the math binder for easy access.

Children need to practice the various strategies before they truly understand them. In Chapter 7, an explanation on using a problem solving journal is given. In that journal, students should have an example of each type of problem they are solving. This becomes an excellent reference for students to use whenever they are attempting to solve new problems, but have forgotten some of the strategies.

Chapter 6 will offer ideas on how to make the most of the word problems by modifying the ones students have already solved. This is useful for helping students who are having difficulty with a problem as well as challenging students who have finished their work early. Being able to modify previously solved word problems will also offer the teachers the opportunity to check their students' progress. Repeated practice is needed to master problem solving skills, but sometimes the text is limited for such repeated practice.

"If a child can't learn the way we teach,
maybe we should teach the way they learn."
Ignacio Estrada

Chapter 6

How to Get the Most Out of the Word Problems

There are many ways to use a word problem. Some of those ways have been discussed previously. One way was to use word problems for teaching the students how to locate the question. Locating the question can be difficult especially if the word problem is lengthy or if the question is really in a statement form. Another way to use word problems was to show the completed work for discussions on, "Does that answer make sense?". A third way was to show students examples of word problems for each type of strategy so they can get a "mental picture on what to look for when deciding which strategy to use. Next, teachers can use word problems to teach students how to look for key words.

However, there are other ways to use the same word problems. Below, there is a word problem that was previously used in Chapter 5. This chapter will demonstrate how that same word problem can be utilized over and over so teachers can obtain the maximum effect of problems. This is useful to know since some students might need their word problems rewritten for better understanding of the problems, whereas other students might need more challenging problems. Sometimes teachers might want to use the original word problem to teach the strategy, and then modify the same problem to see if the students can solve it on their own. Also, being able to modify problems from the text offers the teachers more word problems to use.

Original word problem

Maria loves shopping. She loves to shop so much that she drives to the Senator Mall once a week. Two weeks ago, Maria visited seven stores, but only made purchases at two.

First, Maria went to Music City, a place that specializes in all items of music. She browsed for 2 hours before making a decision on what to buy. At the checkout counter, she had 3 CDs that were priced at $10.99 each and 1 second hand CD priced at $5.95. During this time, she gave the sales associate 2 twenty dollar bills.

Maria went to Girls' Boutique where she tried on five blouses, three skirts, and eight necklaces. After some careful thinking, she decided on three blouses which cost $21.99, $18.50, and $26.99. She also bought two skirts which cost $35.99 each. How much money did she spend at this store?

The above multistep problem can be modified or extended in the following ways.

Change the numbers

Changing the numbers would be a great way to modify the problem so struggling students would be able to work on the same problem as the rest of the class. Then too, teachers might want to see if students can remember how to solve the problem, but with different numbers.

First, Maria went to Music City, a place that specializes in all items of music. She browsed for 2 hours before making a decision on what to buy. At the checkout counter, she had 3 CDs that were priced at $10 each and 1 second hand CD priced at $5. During this time, she gave the sales associate two twenty dollar bills. How much change should Maria receive from the cashier?

By eliminating the cents part of each number, the problem has been simplified for the struggling students without changing the gist of the problem. Changing how many of an item can increase the difficulty level while the basic problem remains the same. Below, the number of CDs had been adjusted.

First, Maria went to Music City, a place that specializes in all items of music. She browsed for 2 hours before making a decision on what to buy. At the checkout counter, she had 4 CDs that were priced at $10.98 each and 2 second hand CDs priced at $5.95 a piece. During this time, she gave the sales associate 3 twenty dollar bills.

Change the setting of the problem

Changing the location for Maria's shopping as well as what she purchased can help the teacher see if the students are learning how to search for clues. Since Maria is buying computer games, the prices can be higher. The basic strategy for solving this problem is the same, but the setting and even the numbers are different. By changing the setting, the problem is showing the students how real world situations are related.

Maria went to Computer Land where people can find all sorts of computer games. She wanted to get her brother some games for his birthday. Since her brother loves sports, she bought 2 sports games at $32.85 a piece. If she gave the cashier $100, how much money would she have left?

Change the strategy

The teacher can use the above new setting, but adjust it so the students have to use an organized list to find the solution. Often, when the teacher cannot locate problems for various strategies, he/she might want to revisit recently used problems to see if they can be rewritten.

Maria went to Computer Land where people can find all sorts of computer games at various prices. She wanted to buy some games for her brother's birthday. Since he loves sports, she decided to check into games with sports as the theme. She found two different price levels. One set of sports games was selling for $24.95 each. The second group of games was selling for $32.85 a piece. Maria wanted to find out how many games she could buy for $100. Figure out the combinations of sports games at the two prices. Remember, her total could not be over $100. She could be just under, but not over. You also need to remember that she was buying games under two different price categories. The students would need to construct a chart such as the one below.

How many of each game could she buy and still be under $100?

$24.95	$32.85	Total
1	1	$57.80
2	1	$82.75
1	2	$90.65
2	2	$115.60
3	1	$107.70

Change the problem by switching what was given and what needs to be solved

Instead of having to find out how much money the cashier should give her for change, this problem now asks how many games Maria purchased. The students may need an organized list again because they have to determine how many games she bought, or the students might decide to use division to see how many times $32.85 will go into $100. The students could even use guess and test strategy to see if they can find the number of games purchased. However they still have to keep in mind that Maria receives $34.30 from the cashier. The thinking process is different simply because the given information and what needs to be solved was changed.

Maria went to Computer Land where people can find all sorts of computer games. She wanted to get her brother some games for his birthday. Since her brother loves sports, she bought some sports games at $32.85 a piece. When she gave the cashier $100, she received $34.30. How many games did she buy?

Change or add a condition

First, Maria went to Music City, a place that specializes in all items of music. She browsed for 2 hours before making a decision on what to buy. At the checkout counter, she had 4 CDs that were priced at $10.98 each and 2 second hand CDs priced at $5.95 a piece. During this time, she gave the sales associate 3 twenty dollar bills.

How much money did the cashier give her?

The condition was that Maria bought CDs from two different price groups. The word problem could also have had the given and wanted switched as a result of adding another price category.

Maria went to Music City, a place that specializes in all items of music. She browsed for 2 hours before making a decision on what to buy. At the checkout counter, she had 4 CDs that were at $10.98 a piece, 3 CDs at $25 each, and 2 second hand CDs priced at $5.95 each. If Maria had $200 in her purse, how much money will she have left after she purchased the different CDs?

Change the problem using a combination of changes.

Maria went to Music City, a place that specializes in all items of music. She browsed for 2 hours before making a decision on what to buy. At the checkout counter, she had 5 CDs that were priced at $15.50 each and 3 second hand CDs priced at $5.95 a piece. Maria has $95 in her handbag.

"Have you got a problem? Do what you can where you are with what you've got."
Theodore Roosevelt

Chapter 7

Problem Solving Journal

Why should students keep a problem solving journal? Having the students create a problem solving journal will give them an extra resource to use whenever they face difficult problems or forget how to solve problems similar to the ones they have solved at an earlier time. This journal should contain a few examples of each skill that is taught, but the teacher should not expect the students to include every single problem they had solved.

The students should have the key words highlighted as well as a written explanation on how they solved the problem. Some of these could be done by the whole class or in small groups using chart paper or transparencies. After the sharing of ideas and discussion, students then copy the work.

This journal could be a useful tool when the students come across a problem that seems difficult yet familiar to them. They can skim through the journal to find similar problems and look over their work.

What should be included in the journal? The problems should be examples of word problems the class has been working on. The students should have the key words highlighted. There should be an example word problem for each strategy that is being taught at the students' given grade level. Both the students and the teacher can identify which problems should be in the journal. Students could also have writing prompts in the problem solving journal so long as the prompts deal with word problems.

Sometimes the problem can be done by the whole class. The teacher could have chart paper on the board or use the overhead projector. If the students are copying from the board or the overhead, the teacher might have some copies already created for the students who have difficulty in taking notes.

For a different way, the teacher could have the word problem on multiple copies, cut into strips, and have the students either glue or staple the strip onto one of the sheets in the journal. If the students had worked on a particularly difficult or complex word problem and one student did an exceptional job, the teacher might to ask that child's permission for sharing the work with the class in the journal.

A homework assignment might be to have the students share with their parents the problem that was done that day. Then the parent initial or sign the page. This way, the parents can see what is being done in the classroom plus have a guide on how the students do their work.

By having the students keep a journal of previously solved word problems and examples of writing prompts dealing with word problems, they have created a reference guide. This guide can be useful in helping students become more willing to try various problems and learn perseverance. They could even use this journal during the summer vacation for review or use it the following year. This journal is useful when the students encounter a word problem that looks familiar, but they cannot remember how to solve it. Being able to look up previously solved word problems can be comforting and conducive to learning new skills. The journal also becomes useful when students are concerned about what to write for the word problem prompts. The teacher should keep a copy of the problem solving journal for the "classroom" in case there is a new student, someone was absent, or if someone misplaces their own copy.

"Many children struggle in schools . . . because the way they are being taught is incompatible with the way they learn." Peter Senge

Chapter 8

Math Anxiety: Causes and Prevention

Trevor was a healthy seven-year-old in the second grade. He was generally excited about school because he was learning about so many things. For example, he had learned about the polar regions of the world and how the weather affects animals. He loved penguins and polar bears. The more he learned about them, the more he loved school.

When he entered third grade, Trevor was still excited about school. Reading was exciting and so was science and social studies. Then math time arrived. Something happened to Trevor. After a few weeks, his heart rate started to increase, he would break into a sweat, and he would feel weak whenever it was time for math instruction. Instead of being that happy seven-year-old, Trevor became fearful of school.

His mother did not understand what happened to her son. The previous year, he was happy and having a good time learning during math instruction. His second grade teacher said he was always one of the first students to finish his work. He was eager to raise his hand to answer questions. However, now he was one of the last to complete his work and seldom raised his hand to volunteer. In the morning, when it was time to go to school, Trevor would start having cramps in his stomach. **What caused this big change from second grade to third?**

Could there be differences between the textbook used in the second grade and the one used in third grade? In many school systems, the textbook for second grade has very large print and large numbers. Each page consists of problems to do, but for word problems there were plus or minus signs already in place. The numbers were always in the same place in the word problems. All Trevor had to do was to fill in the numbers from the problems. In other words, for the subtraction problems, the larger number was always first and the number with the lesser value was always second. This was just perfect for filling in the problem. The basic format rarely changed. Even the worksheets the teacher had used were using the same format. Children also wrote in the math book. Sometimes they copied off of the board but not too often.

However, the third grade textbook was thicker in size, the print was smaller, and the word problems were different. The format was different each time the students were presented with new word problems to solve, and the signs were not printed. Also, the numbers were not in the same pattern. Sometimes the larger ones were first, and sometimes they were last. The students had to copy the problems onto to their papers as the students were no longer permitted to write in their books!

In third grade, there was also pressure to complete more difficult assignments and practice for the big test. Trevor kept hearing about that big test many times. In all fairness to his third grade teacher, she did not choose the math text, nor did she choose to prepare for the big test. She was under a great deal of pressure to prepare the children.

This story was just one scenario describing how students might become anxious in math class. There are other causes leading to math anxiety.

What is math anxiety? What are other causes of math anxiety? How can the adults help children who are experiencing this problem? Mathematics anxiety has been defined as feelings of tension and worry. It often interferes with manipulation of numbers as well as the solving of math problems not only in school, but also in real life situations. This anxiety can cause students to forget what had just been taught and even lose one's self confidence (Tobias, 1993). Math anxiety causes students to become obsessive with the feeling that "everyone knows that I don't understand" (Tobias, 1993). "I'd better not draw attention to myself by asking questions" (Stuart, 2000). Keep in mind that asking questions is one of the things students should do when they do not understand a math concept or a math procedure. This feeling of uneasiness and fear about math matters can remain all through adult life.

What are some of the **symptoms** of math anxiety? Children with math anxiety might experience headaches, queasy stomachs, sweaty palms, and a dry mouth.

Math anxiety can lead to math avoidance or even math phobia. For example, there is the story about Justin, a fourth grader. He experienced math anxiety so badly, that just before math class he would "need to use the bathroom in a hurry", forced himself to throw up, and then asked to see the nurse. At first, his teacher honestly thought he was sick, but soon she and the nurse began to realize this was much more serious. After observing his behavior and work habits during the first few weeks into the school year, the teacher realized this child needed testing for a possible learning disability.

Finally, Justin was tested. The analysis of the various tests proved he did have learning disabilities that interfered with his memory skills as well as the ability to make sense of what he read and wrote. In reading class, he was already in a group for below average students and he worked at a somewhat slower pace than the other two groups.

However, the memory skills played a serious role in his poor recall of basic math facts and needing several reminders on how to multiply and divide. The low leveled-reading interfered with his ability to solve word problems. His writing skills interfered with his math journal writing assignments as well as when he had to explain how he solved problems.

The resource teacher and the classroom teacher worked cooperatively to find ways to help him cope with math and even find success in math class. They placed him with other students with similar difficulties with reading and writing. That way they could work on those two skills using various strategies that will be explained later on in this book. At the end of the year, this child was a lot happier about his ability to read and solve math problems. He still had some difficulties, but at least he felt he could be part of the class and actually understand the word problems.

Not only can learning disabilities affect students, but teachers' attitude can affect the students as well. "Teachers, probably second to parents, are students' most important influence in how they view math" (Jackson and Leffingwell 1999). Jackson and Leffingwell discovered in their research that there were three categories of grade levels where math anxiety occurs:

1. Elementary level, grades 3 and 4
2. High School level, grades 9-11
3. College level, freshman year

In fourth grade, the level of difficulty increases dramatically. Students are taking timed tests and competing against each other to see who is the fastest. Math concepts being taught in the fourth grade are more difficult. Memorizing multiplication and division tables as well as formulas such as finding the area of a rectangle are extremely important to meeting with success in fourth grade math. Not only do students face an increase in the pressure on what they have to learn, but their teachers may become upset if they ask for help because they are expecting more of the students. Some teachers even point out their mistakes in front of the entire class.

The next group who may encounter math anxiety is in high school in grades 9-11. Teachers may become angry when asked for help. They may even say aloud that the students should have mastered those skills the first time they were introduced to them. Many of these students even remember having to go to the chalkboard to go over a problem until it is finished and still not comprehend what they did.

The last group where math anxiety can happen is during students' freshman year at the college level. Professors generally lecture and have very little interaction with the students. If students ask questions, they may be demeaned for not having the prerequisite skills. Professors may even dislike having to teach the entry level math classes and have little patience for anyone needing extra help.

Math anxiety can be caused by other factors as well. When students are not encouraged to become involved in the class, they become disconnected from the subject. If they do not feel comfortable in asking questions, then they are unable to find clarity in their understanding of the concepts. When teachers teach math only as rules and symbols, students see math as a separate entity that has to be learned, but "there is no use for." If students have to start a new concept before the previous one has been learned, then the next skill will more than likely not be mastered since math is built up from previously learned ideas and concepts. This happens more frequently because teachers must stay with the master timeline and scope of sequence. Quite often taking another day to teach or even review previously taught concepts are frowned upon since it will deviate from the time frame preceding the major tests all schools have to administer.

Teachers have mandated state curriculum that must be covered in a certain amount of time. Often teachers feel they do not have adequate time to answer students' questions and are pressured to go by chapter by chapter. Teachers, administrators, and the curriculum designers need to cooperatively work on ways to adjust the curriculum to meet the needs of all students.

Teachers and parents may have preconceived notions concerning who can learn mathematical concepts better: girls or boys. When girls have parents or teachers who feel that only the boys can do well in math, and are given less help than the boys, they tend not to do as well as they could have. When girls are expected to do as well as boys and are given the opportunity to succeed in math, they excel quite well.

Sometimes math anxiety can begin in school, but many times it can commence at home. Parents and guardians possess a great influence over children which is a great thing. However, if those same parents and guardians had experienced difficulties in math, they might just impart their negative feelings about math onto the children. How? When parents express ideas like, "I was never good at math" or "math was hard for me, so I don't expect my child to be able to understand it either", they impart their fear of math onto their children. Many parents might have unpleasant memories about their own math experiences, but that does not imply their children cannot do well in math. Parents need to encourage their children to do well no matter how difficult math was for them when they were in school. Also, they need to seek advice and assistance from the teachers and even the guidance counselors. Guidance counselors could provide advice on how to assist their children without transferring their fear of math. Teachers could offer ideas on how parents can help their children at home during homework and even during the summer. Sometimes it helps the teachers to know where the child's anxious feelings have originated.

On the other hand, if the parents were extremely good at math, they might not comprehend why their children are having difficulty in class and might even express thoughts like "What's wrong with you? I did well in math and so should you." "You just need to try harder." "I am so disappointed in you." If children are repeatedly having difficulty in math, perhaps they have a math learning disability, math anxiety, or perhaps they just need the parents' understanding that not everyone in the family will excel in math, but everyone can learn. Some students require certain skills repeatedly strengthened before those skills are mastered.

Another cause of math anxiety could be that the students do not feel confident about their abilities in math. Perhaps the vocabulary and reading passages are above the students' level of understanding. Some of these students could have a learning disability that centers on math. Memory skills, being able to pay attention to instruction, organizational skills and even reading and writing skills can all affect how a student feels about solving word problems.

In summary, students may face math anxiety due to the following factors.

- Prior negative experiences with math
- Bad grade school and/or high school teachers
- Lack of encouragement from parents and teachers
- Lack of positive role models
- Gender bias
- Pressure felt by taking timed tests
- Constant testing
- Fear of looking or feeling stupid in front of peers
- Students placed in wrong ability level in math courses
- Prerequisite concepts either lacking or not fully mastered
- Little or lack of encouragement to ask questions to help clarify what is being taught

What are some possible strategies for preventing math anxiety?

Parent and teachers need to be aware of their attitudes in math. If they show how they might be anxious in math, then their children and students will pick up on this and begin to be anxious as well. On the other hand, if parents and teachers expect the children to master skills before they are ready to do so, math anxiety can set in.

Students need to be encouraged to become active learners rather than passive learners. Instead of sitting at their desks listening to lectures, students should be encouraged to ask questions and risk trying out challenges without thinking they will be ridiculed. A positive atmosphere should be established both in school and at home. This does not mean that children are given A's simply by asking questions. High standards can still be maintained in a positive climate.

Teachers need to and often do apprise parents of any difficulties the children might have in learning concepts. Schools might want to develop a tutoring service where students who have mastered the required skills can tutor students who need help. This can strengthen the skills as well as foster cooperativeness among peers.

If the parents are notified about the concepts and skills their children are lacking, they need to be active in searching for ideas on how to help their children. It is necessary for children to practice basic skills not only during school, but also during the summer to strengthen those skills taught during the year. If they have a computer and Internet hook up at home, then the parents can have their children use those programs that specialize on practicing basic math skills. There are even websites that specialize in creating worksheets for basic math skills, algebra, and geometry. Some of those websites are listed in the Appendix. Parents might look into a tutor for their children if they are uncomfortable with the skills or perhaps they have never even had that level of math.

Questioning is very important to ensure that the problem solving process continues and is not halted by a lack of ideas (Nitert, 1996). If students seem stumped by the problem or if they are not use to the particular type of strategy needed to solve the problem, then they might give up before the lesson even starts. However, if the problem solving activity is a review, teachers and parents have to be careful about how much information the questioning is drawing out.

Various learning styles need to be addressed in the classroom. Often the math teachers might have a learning style that is not the same as the students. That is understandable since there are such a variety of learning styles. However, the teachers need to be responsive to this and search out ways to accommodate all of the learning styles in their classrooms. There are surveys that students can fill out to give the teachers a better idea what those learning styles might be. Various techniques can be used to address various learning styles during any given lesson.

Cooperative groups should be used whenever possible to ensure that all students are actively engaged in their learning. Numbered Heads Together, Think-Pair-Share, and Think-Pair-Write-Share help children experiencing reading and writing difficulties. These cooperative learning techniques assist all students when a new strategy has been introduced or if they are reviewing for a test. Numbered Heads Together is further explained in Chapter 3. Think-Pair-Share and Think-Pair-Write-Share are further explained in Chapter 10.

Differentiated instruction, such as tiered activities, rewriting the problems, projects, and anchored activities, assist all learners whether they are below average, on grade level, or needing the extra challenge. Teachers need to find ways to aid students who have not mastered prerequisite concepts. This can be accomplished via differentiated instruction as well as using technology in the classroom. There are several websites that offer students extra practice in skills essential to understanding mathematics.

Teachers and parents need to demonstrate to children how math is connected to other subjects as well as the real world. Realizing that math is crucial to everyday life as well as their potential future actually makes math very important to them. When they are involved in such activities, they become more immersed in mathematics.

"The essence of mathematics is not to make simple things complicated, but to make complicated things simple." S. Gudder.

Chapter 9

What To Do If Students Are Experiencing Difficulty in Understanding the Word Problem

There are many factors that attribute to poor problem solving. For the literacy issues, there might be little understanding of mathematical vocabulary, limited ability to read the problems, and limited verbal ability to explain thinking. For number sense issues, there might be difficulty in focusing on important information, limited ability to picture the situation, and limited self-checking ability. As for the instructional issues, there might be limited personal appeal and limited time to solve problems (Sherman, Richardson, Yard, 2009). There are also problem solving difficulty factors (factors within the physical problems that cause difficulty) such as numbers presented in the wrong order, key words, extra words, hidden word numbers, implied numbers, multiple steps, and exact mathematical vocabulary (Mink, 2009)

If children are having a great deal of difficulty in understanding the problem, try:

- Rewriting the problem on their comprehension level
- Reading the problem aloud
- Practicing their mathematics vocabulary
- Picturing the problem in their mind
- Breaking the problem down in smaller parts
- Allowing the use of manipulatives
- Having the students role play the problem
- Repeating a problem, but change the numbers
- Guiding them to a similar problem that has already been successfully solved
- Questioning them about the different parts
- Teaching the student about using a problem solving model that meets their needs

Rewriting word problems so students can read them

One reason some students may have difficulty in solving word problems may be their comprehension is not on grade level. Perhaps they are unable to handle too many details at one time. In either case, the word problems can be rewritten to see if that helps. If it does, then their math skills are fine, but their comprehension is holding them back. When rewriting the word problems that are written in a paragraph form, the teacher might want to leave spaces between each section of the problem. Keeping a record of the rewritten problems will help the teacher next year.

Read the problem aloud

Rather than rewriting the word problem, the teacher could read the problem aloud. Often this helps the students understand what is expected and what is happening in the problem. This could even assist the students who are auditory learners. For these auditory learners, they could even read their problems "aloud in their minds" so no one in class will be disturbed. This technique is frequently utilized in reading class. Why not utilize it in mathematics?

Practicing mathematic vocabulary

Teachers need to ensure that students' lack of comprehension is not due to their math vocabulary. If that is the case, then math vocabulary skills should be practiced. Part of students' homework assignments could be to review their math dictionary each night, complete a crossword puzzle, do a matching activity, or even label the parts of a problem. Refer to Chapter 3 for more details on creating the math dictionary which can be used in school and at home.

Parents want to be involved in their children's math, but quite often do not know what to do since they were taught so differently. Having the vocabulary section can assist parents a great deal.

Picturing in one's mind

People use mental pictures all of the time. As people attempt to remember a favorite holiday, meal, or vacation, they often close their eyes so they can revisit that memory. When people are cooking, building, planting, or shopping, they use mental imagery. They picture in their minds what those clothes will look like in another color, how that special meal will appear on the dining room table, which arrangement for the garden would be more appealing, and how the new paint color will change the room's atmosphere.

Teachers and parents can have children close their eyes as the adults reread the problem out loud to them. As they read each section slowly, both teachers and parents can guide children in what they are seeing in their minds.

For example:

Tom was watching birds that came to the backyard feeder. He kept track of how many he saw each day. For Sunday, Tom saw 12 birds, 1 squirrel, and one cat come to the bird feeder. On Monday, he saw 5 birds. Tuesday, he saw 8 birds and one cat. Then on Wednesday, he spotted 8 more birds and three squirrels. For Thursday and Friday, he noticed that 6 birds and 2 squireels came each day. Last, he recorded 9 birds for Saturday.

How many birds did Tom see during that week?

For the above problem, the students should read the problem by themselves twice. As the children read the problem the second time, they should highlight key words and numbers. Then the teachers should read the problem out loud as the children close their eyes and picture what is happening. Afterwards, step by step, the adults ask the children questions about what they pictured.

Below are some questions that could assist the children in analyzing the problem.

What was Tom doing? Where is Tom? How many days did Tom watch the birds? How many birds did he see on Sunday? Monday? Tuesday? Wednesday? Thursday? Friday? Saturday? Did he see anything else? Does that information help you solve the problem? Why or why not? What is the problem asking you to solve?

After the adults and children discuss the word problem, the children choose a strategy to solve the problem.

Breaking down the problem into smaller parts

Here's an example of how to help children break a problem down into smaller parts.

Problem: John has a target board made out of vinyl material. There were three balls made of sticky material like that found on Velcro fasteners. On the target there are three ways to score. In the center there is a 2" square made out of Velcro. That square is worth 100 points. On the outside there are pink circles and large green squares. The 4 pink circles are worth 50 points. The smaller green squares are worth 20 points.

Find the highest score using 3 balls. Then find the lowest score using 3 balls. Each time, all of the balls were attached to the target.

How many combinations of scoring can you find? Make a chart to show the combinations. Show your work.

After children read the problem at least twice and highlight key words and numbers, teachers assist the children's comprehension of the problem by breaking it down into smaller parts through questioning the students such as:

- What game does John have?
- What is the object of that game?
- How do you score?
- What happens if a ball lands on the center square?
- What happens if a ball lands on one of the larger squares?
- What happens if a ball lands on one of the pink circles?
- How many tries do you have to get a final score?
- How can you find out what would be the highest score using all three balls?
- How can you find out what would be the lowest score using all three balls?
- Are there any numbers in the problem that you do not need to use? Why not? Cross them out.
- What do you need to do in order to have an organized way of showing your work?

The questions facilitate the students' understanding of the problem because they break down the problem. For each question, the students discuss with their partners or small groups the answers. This technique is especially good when students are assigned a problem using an unfamiliar situation since the discussions add to their prior knowledge and clarify portions of the problem they do not understand. However, teachers should not use this technique unless students are having difficulty with the problem. Sometimes too many questions can decrease the thinking that students should be doing during problem solving activities.

Using manipulatives

Manipulatives can aid students who are visual and/or tactile learners. Sometimes when children have difficulty in understanding the problem, they need to manipulate objects to act out the problem. Even older students in the immediate grades as well as middle school should have access to manipulatives.

For example:

Sara was visiting the local pond with her dad. At the pond were several ducks. Swimming in the pond were five ducks. Walking around the rim of the pond were 8 ducks. Then two feet away were 7 ducks looking for food. How many ducks did Sara see?

Permit children to handle blocks, square tiles, clips, or some other group of manipulatives that would be easy for them to manipulate. After the children have read the problem twice and have highlighted key words and numbers, they should be instructed to draw a diagram of the pond area. The adults need to remind the children that the diagram does not need to be perfect, but rather, a symbol to help them solve the problem. This is important because children often become bogged down in the drawing part since they want the picture to be perfect. Both parents and teachers can ask the following questions as the children manipulate the objects.

How many ducks were swimming on the pond? Then use that many objects on the diagram to represent those ducks.

How many ducks were walking around the rim of the pond? Then use that many objects around the pond to represent those ducks.

How many ducks were two feet away looking for food? Then use that many objects near the pond to represent those ducks.

Now count the objects. How many ducks did Sara see in the pond, around the rim of the pond, and near the pond? Write an equation to show your work.

Role playing the problem

Maria wants to plan a garden of flowers for the backyard. She thinks a garden of 5 feet by 8 feet would be a good size. However, she needs to prepare the ground by adding rich topsoil. How much topsoil would she need to buy if she digs up the ground 5 ft by 8 ft with 3 inches deep? What information is needed in order to solve this problem?

After students read the problem a second time, they can role play what Maria needs to do in order to solve this problem. The students could use yarn to lay out a "garden" in a room or even outside. Actually, people often use string and sticks to map out gardens when they first plan a garden. Once the "garden" has been mapped out, some of the students can pretend they are digging the ground to loosen up the soil 3" deep. Then the children can pretend to "read" the information on a bag of topsoil to determine how many cubic inches each bag covers. What do they need to do now? Students can think of other problems that they have solved that would relate to this one. Last, the students solve the problem, but after doing some research on how much soil is in a certain size bag.

Repeating a problem, but change the numbers

This is an easy technique to do. If students are having some difficulty with a specific type of problem, the teacher could show them one problem on the chalkboard and discuss how to solve it. Then the teacher replaces the numbers to see if the students can solve it on their own. The problem could be left on the board and be revisited the next day for a quick warm-up. The only difference would be different numbers. The goals to revisiting this problem would be to see if the students are thoroughly reading the problem and understanding what to do.

Using a problem solving model that meets the needs of students

Polya's Problem Solving Model could be adapted to suit the needs of students. However, there are other problem solving models that can be located on the Internet or various books on problem solving. Most of those models only work with word problems that require an equation, but there are a few that can be employed while using various problem solving strategies. STARR, which can be found on the Internet, is one that uses an acronym to help students remember the steps. There are some that break down the steps into five or six rather than Polya's four step model. The book, *On Cloud Nine*, was written by Nanci Bell and Kimberly Tulley to assist students with learning disabilities. Using their model requires students to use verbalization and visualization. The important idea to keep in mind is to locate a model or adapt a model to suit the needs of students.

"In reading, writing and oral communication are important aspects of instruction; in math, having students write down and discuss their ideas can help them develop, cement, and extend their understanding." Marilyn Burns

Chapter 10

Using Writing and Reading Strategies to Help Students Understand Word Problems

Communication is vital to strengthened understanding mathematics. When students are permitted to talk their way through a problem, listen to others' doing the same, and write about the steps they took to solve the problem, they are becoming more involved in solving that problem. Through communicating, they are learning how to organize their thoughts and they are strengthening their mathematical thinking skills. Communication is so important that it is one of the five NCTM process standards in mathematics (Silbey, 2002).

Teachers and parents need to use reading and writing strategies to help children understand word problems more clearly. After all, word problems are stories that need to be solved mathematically. If reading and writing strategies can assist students during reading instruction, why not use the same strategies to enhance and strengthen comprehension of the word problems during math instruction?

Activating Prior knowledge

Activating prior knowledge is a wonderful strategy that can be used before the students attempt to solve the word problems. Suppose students are working on a group of word problems related to the circus. Both teachers and parents need to ask questions such as:

- Who has been to a circus?
- What kinds of events happen at the circus?
- How might spectators spend their money?

- How high up do the acrobats perform?
- What do the animals need to eat?
- Can you think of ways that math is used at the circus other than people paying to see the circus?

These questions can awaken memories of some of the children's past experiences with the circus, can stir up memories of children who have read about the circus, can help children who have never heard of a circus. As they discuss these questions and others, they are sharing what they know with their class or group. If the teachers could even ask questions about the strategies needed to solve the problems. To make sure they will not give away the strategies that the children need to use, they can also discuss a few other strategies as well. Again, this discussion will awaken what children already know. **Stirring up prior knowledge is a powerful way to involve the children in what they are reading.**

Numbered heads together

Numbered heads together is a cooperative learning strategy that encourages students to discuss and share ideas. Being able to hear the ideas of other students can help everyone reflect on ideas they had not thought of previously. Being able to say their own ideas aloud and hearing what other students think about those ideas can be a way to motivate involvement and thinking.

Students are arranged in groups of four and are numbered from 1 to 4. The groups discuss a solution to a math word problem. To report back to the class, the teacher chooses a random number, such as 2. For the next time, the teacher can choose another random number. Most of the time, classes do not have a class size that is a multiple of 4. When that happens, the teacher might need to have a group of 5. In that case, two students are assigned with the same number.

Scanning the passage

Scanning is another useful tool for increasing comprehension of a word problem, particularly if that problem is lengthy. It is even listed under Polya's Problem Solving Method. **Good readers ask themselves questions as they read in language arts classes. Why not use that same technique while students scan the word problem?**

By scanning and asking themselves questions while reading a word problem, the students can prepare themselves for reading the problem a second time. During the second reading the students are able to look more carefully for the details that will help them find the solution.

These questions are included in the Appendix. As the students scan the problem, they need to ask themselves:

- What do I understand?
- What is not clear to me?
- Why it is not clear to me?
- What is the problem?
- What needs to be done in order to solve the problem?
- What I do need in order to do that?
- What information is given?
- What information is missing?
- Which details are not needed?

Teachers can model this through a think-aloud. Next, the students can practice using this technique on a few word problems either by themselves or in pairs. Then they could discuss how the act of asking themselves questions during scanning helped prepared them for the second reading. The class discussion is important since the students gain valuable insight from each other on how scanning can facilitate better comprehension of the word problem.

Paraphrasing the word problem

The act of paraphrasing the word problem facilitates the first step in most problem solving models. When students are able to paraphrase the passage, they demonstrate that they really do understand what they had just read. To paraphrase a word problem simply means restating the word problem without changing the meaning and ideas of the initial passage. This reading technique assists the young students and struggling students with checking their understanding of the problem situation. **This is another strategy that good readers use while reading, and it is also useful during math when there are word problems to read.**

The teachers need to model this technique utilizing a think-aloud activity. In this activity, the teachers show the students how to use the facts from the word problem into their own words. After the teachers have shown the students how to paraphrase the passage, the students should practice the technique. They could start with some simple word problems and progress to problems with slightly more information in the passages. Paraphrasing could be done orally or by writing. Students could work on the paraphrasing in pairs or in small groups. After they had had sufficient time to think about what they will say or write, they should share their work with a partner or the small group.

KWL Chart

How many teachers and parents use the KWL chart in reading class? Why not use this chart for the other subjects? However the KWL chart for math is slightly different. The K stands for What I Already Know about the theme of the story. In math, it represents what the students already know about the theme behind the word problems. The W stands for What I Want to Learn about the story in reading class. In math, the W represents What I Need to Know in order to solve the problem. Students need to restate the questions in statement form for this column.

The L stands for What I Have Learned in reading the story. In math, the L represents the solution. Students need to write down what strategy they used plus record how they solved the problem.

Students can easily construct their own KWL chart. All they need to do is to fold the paper into three equal parts. Then they need to write the name of each column. However, they should make sure that their work is neatly done and organized. If this chart is to be used for a series of word problems, then the students should draw a line beneath each problem all across the three columns before they use the chart for the next problem. For younger students or students who have difficulty with hand coordination, a prepared copy of the KWL could be used. If the teacher is utilizing this technique for the first time, then the students should have a prepared copy to write on as the teacher models how to use the chart. Read the word problem on the following page.

Shopping at the Mall

Maria went to Girls' Boutique where she tried on five blouses, three skirts, and eight necklaces. After some careful thinking, she decided on three blouses which cost $21.99, $18.50, and $26.99. She also bought two skirts which cost $35.99 each. How much money did she spend at this store?

The theme for this problem is shopping at the mall. Have the students complete the first column on what they know about shopping and then allow the students to discuss with the class what they wrote. Here is a sample of a KWL chart with the columns filled in to give teachers an idea how the students might fill one out.

What I Already Knew	What I Need to Learn	What I Have Learned
Maria bought three blouses at different prices. The prices were $21.99, $18.99, and $26.99. She bought two skirts costing $35.99 each. When I show my work, I need to make sure the decimal points are lined up if I am adding or subtracting.	How much money Maria spent at the store?	Writing an equation $21.99 + $18.99+$26.99 = $67.98 $67.98 + ($35.99) x 2 = $139.46 Maria spent $139.46 at the store.

This chart is a great organizer to use in math class because it is easy for the students to construct and easy to complete. However, teachers need to model how to construct and use the KWL chart in math. Never should teachers assume that the students will automatically know what to do. Eventually, the students will only use this chart for lengthy problems or difficult problems.

The first time a KWL chart is used in math, teachers should apply the Think-aloud strategy to teach the students how to use this method of exploring the problem. Allowing the students to hear the teachers think aloud on how they would use the chart for a problem is a powerful way to initialize their usage of this chart.

If the teachers and students are doing this together, they could discuss what each student wrote. On a larger version of this chart the teachers would write what the children are sharing with the class. Perhaps the students could be in pairs and complete this work together, or the students could work with pairs on the first two columns and complete the last column on their own.

Visualize images or pictures in your minds from the word problem

Good readers use mental images as they read a book, a short story, nonfiction selection, and even brochures. **Why not use visualizing images in math class?** When students visualize a passage from the word problem, they are creating pictures in their minds. Students create these images using details from the word problem during and after reading. These mental pictures are used to support their grasp of the problem's text.

Teachers could model the process of creating images. Either the teachers could read aloud the passage or have one of the students do the reading aloud. The teachers could even close their eyes or stare out as they are busily making these images. As they form these mental images, they need to describe what they are seeing so the students can compare the teachers' mental images with the written text.

The next step in teaching this strategy would be to have the students in pairs so they can practice making mental images. While one student reads aloud the passage from a word problem, the other student closes his eyes to form the mental image. Afterwards, he describes in detail his "picture" so his partner can check with the word problem to make sure the picture is accurate and not missing any important details.

Teachers could post the question: What pictures or images did you see in your mind as you read the word problem? Then have a class discussion.

Coding the text

Students need to self-monitor as they read if they are going to be independent in the problem solving. The self-monitoring is also needed for the students in checking their understanding and choosing a fix-up strategy if they require one. Coding the text is one strategy that helps students work towards independently choosing fix-up strategy. It helps the students generate questions about the passage. Coding the text also helps to develop the students' metacognitive skills. This strategy helps students deal with confusing portions of the passage.

Before the students can do coding the text on their own, the teacher needs to perform a think-aloud. In this way, the students have a model for using this strategy. During the strategy, the students utilize sticky notes to mark the portions in the problem that are confusing and things they want to know more about.

The codes:

?	I am confused/I don't understand
M	I want to learn more about this
*	This is important
N	New information
C	Connection
TH	Theme of the text
AHA	Big idea in the text

Developing readers or struggling students should be limited to the first two codes which are important for the readers understanding. The more fluent readers can use the rest of the codes. The teacher could create a poster that shows the various codes that the children will be using. This poster should be prominently displayed in the room. A personal copy for each student would be beneficial as well. A copy of the chart is included in the Appendix.

For practice, the teacher could have another word problem on chart paper posted on the wall for all to see. Each student should have a copy of the same word problem. The students could be in pairs or in groups. As they read the selection by themselves, they employ the sticky notes. They also practice generating questions for further understanding. Then the students share with their partner or partners where they placed the sticky notes and explain the reasons why they did. Through this partner discussion, they are giving each other the opportunity to gain further understanding as well as "hearing" the thinking of their classmates. For further reading about using reading strategies in math class, teachers might want to use the book, *Reading Strategies for Mathematics* written by Trisha Brummer and Stephanie Macceca, published by Shell Education, 2004. ISBN-978-1-4258-0055-0.

Writing in math class

Writing has been incorporated in math class for the following reasons. First of all, students think about their learning which is an important step to their true understanding of the math concepts. Second, writing in math strengthens students' knowledge of important concepts by explaining and giving examples of those concepts. Third, students create connections between real world applications and the word problems they are solving. Next, having the students write about what they have learned in math helps the teacher assess how well the students have achieved an understanding of vital concepts and processes. Although writing in mathematics is helpful to both the students and the teachers, it may be difficult to implement this practice. Teachers need to look for simple and easy ways to weave writing activities into the math lesson.

Think-Pair-Share

For students who have difficulty with the writing portion of the math lesson, Think-Pair-Share might be the perfect lead to writing. These same students often have less difficulty in telling the teacher what they think and why they use a certain strategy in problem solving. These students may benefit from sharing their thoughts and reasons with a partner. They also benefit from hearing what the partner has to say. Practicing in pairs before speaking to the whole class is a plus for struggling learners. These students can also choose to share their thoughts, their partner's thoughts, or a combination of the two.

The basic steps of Think-Pair-Share are:

- **Question**: Ask an open-ended question or use a writing prompt. Explain to the students that they will think-pair-share the answer. Keep this question or prompt posted for all to see
- **Think**: Give students 1 to 2 minutes to think quietly about their response to the question. Walk around the room to reinforce this quiet, on-task response.
- **Pair**: Ask students to share their thoughts with their partners and ask questions if they do not understand what their partner is saying. Circulate around the room, listening to student conversations.
- **Share**: Ask for student volunteers to share their ideas. Later, teachers should call on non-volunteers to increase student accountability in this cooperative learning strategy. Reinforce the expectation of active listening by requiring students to acknowledge the thoughts of classmates by saying:

  - *I agree with [name's] answer because . . . ,*
  - *I don't agree with [name's] answer because . . . ,*
  - *I started the problem like [name] but then I . . .*

Think-Write-Pair-Share

After the students have demonstrated proficiency in Think-Pair-Share, teachers could introduce the Think-Write-Pair-Share strategy. Writing is now a component of this strategy. As students think about the question, they also write their response to the question.

Once again, the teachers need to model this strategy. Using a think-aloud as the teachers go through the writing process helps the students assimilate how to perform this task. The teachers could even have a student as the partner. The teacher and student could take turns being the reader and being the listener.

When students work on this strategy, they have the opportunity to share their writings with their partners. During this time, the students can edit their own written responses. As they orally share, they can choose to replace certain words with more appropriate mathematical vocabulary. When students do this, it is exciting to the teachers because it means the students are becoming more acclimated to math vocabulary. After listening to their partner's written responses, students might even add ideas and statements from their partner's writing. **Students learn from each other.**

Finally the teacher can call on some students to share written responses with the class. During this time, a variety of levels of expertise should be chosen for the sharing. The sharing time promotes that all students have something worthy to say and share. This process encourages students to get something down on paper and allows them some editing time. Additionally, students benefit from regular listening to classmates sharing their own writing. The more writing samples students get to listen to, the more they learn about the writing process.

Guided response strategy

For the guided response strategy, the students rewrite a word problem in their own words. Then they create a written plan that can be used to solve that problem. Next, the students solve the problem and then compose an analysis about the strategy that was used (McGehe, 1991).

When this strategy is used for the first time, it should be modeled. The teacherr demonstrates how to apply the guided response strategy by using chart paper and thinking-aloud as the teacher works on the problem. For some students who are struggling with the analysis portion, the teacher can have them work on the rewriting the problem, write about why they chose a certain strategy, and solve the problem. Then compose the analysis with them.

Problem writing

For problem writing, students create and write math problems for the skills being learned in class. Before students write their own math problems, they need to say aloud their word problems. Then the teacher writes what they said either on an overhead transparency or on chart paper. If they seem to be struggling with the oral part, then they should work in teams so the teams can develop a word problem together so each student will be able to say aloud their problem as the teacher calls on each team. The teams have to make sure each person can say the problem aloud because they will not know who the teacher will call on to report the work. Once the class feels comfortable with verbalizing the problems, then they write the problems.

Sample prompts:

- Write an addition problem that has a 3 digit number for the answer.
- Write a math problem to go with a picture.
- Write a story problem that involves multiplication and subtraction.
- Write and illustrate a story problem for a 2nd grader (McGehe, 1991).
- Write a step-by-step explanation of how to solve an equation or graph a function for a student who was absent.

Explanations

After the students solve a problem, they can write an explanation on how they solved it. They could write a "how to "report for another student (Burns, 2004; Fortescue, 1994; Brandenburg, 2002; Evans, 1984).

Troubleshooting

In troubleshooting, the students explain their errors on a particular problem. Before they do one on their own, the teacher models the process using think-aloud and chart paper. Next, the students are assigned an example of mistakes for them to write about. By giving them all the same mistakes to write about, the students will be able to work in teams and listen to each other's explanation. When they are given the opportunity to compare their answers with their peers, they discover what they might be missing in their own explanation. Eventually, the students will be able to explain their errors on their own. There should always be an example prepared for someone to solve in case that student did not make any errors the day this task is assigned. Can the students spot the problem that was correctly solved?

Math pal

Each class could develop a pen pal community. The students could either be writing to pen pals in the same class, in different classes from the same grade, or different schools. They could work on writing word problems or writing explanations. This activity gives the teachers and students the opportunity to incorporate technology. Some students may benefit from using a computer if their handwriting is not very legible while others will like the fact they are writing to an actual audience other than their own classmates (Tichenor & Jewell, 2001).

Writing prompts

Writing prompts can either be short or more involved writing assignments depending upon the goal of the teacher. Short writing assignments would be great for practicing for state tests as well as sparking the thinking processes. They are really rather easy to create, especially If the teachers are using a math problem as a springboard for the short prompt. The more involved writing assignments could be a way to integrate math with other subjects. Quite often the more involved assignments are part of an integrated performance task.

Here are some examples of the short writing assignments which are included in the Appendix.

Problem #1

Marjorie made a sandwich for her lunch at work. She used two slices of bread at 65 calories each. She spread 1 tablespoon of margarine at 101 calories. Next she added 1 slice of cheese at 101 calories and a slice of meat at 161 calories. How many calories were in her sandwich?

Prompt 1

If someone solved the problem with an answer of 49 calories, would that answer make sense? Explain your answer.

Prompt 2

How do you find the number of calories for the two slices of bread being used in the above problem?

Prompt 3

Explain how you would make a sandwich using the same items, but the sandwich has less than 250 calories.

Prompt 4

For the problem, write the question in a statement form.

Each of the 4 prompts is related to the aforementioned problem, yet each one entails a different math skill.

Refer to the Appendix for these prompts.

"What we share in common makes us human. How we differ makes us individuals. In a differentiated classroom, commonalities are acknowledged and built upon, and student differences become important elements in teaching and learning as well." Carol Ann Tomlinson, 2001

Chapter 11

Differentiating Math Instruction

All students have the right to a sound, challenging mathematics curriculum that is taught by mathematic teachers who are knowledgeable and skilled. Those same teachers also need to be well-supported by the administration and the board of education in their respective school districts.

Some students may need more than an impressive math program and excellent teaching to meet high expectations. Students who are experiencing difficulty may benefit from such resources as after-school programs, tutoring, and peer mentoring. Whenever feasible, such students would benefit from cooperative learning and study groups. Students with special learning needs in mathematics should be supported by both their classroom teachers and special education staff. Also, students with exceptional interests or outstanding talent in mathematics may need enrichment programs or additional resources to challenge, highly motivate, and actively involve them in learning.

Differentiated instruction is a process where teachers boost learning by implementing instruction and assessment that is consistent with their students' needs and skill levels. This type of instruction includes a variety of strategies which ensures these students succeed with the same curriculum by providing entry points, learning tasks, and outcomes that are customized to students' needs, yet meaningful and worthwhile.

Differentiated instruction includes lessons:

- for all learners in the class of all levels of abilities and readiness
- for various learning styles
- that is engaging, respectful, and challenging for all levels

- that allows for diversity in students
- that promotes rigor, relevance, and relationships
- that varies the content, process, or product
- that gives flexibility to the curriculum

Centers

Teachers can construct centers on problem solving that can meet the needs of all the students. Centers are not just for the primary grades. They are quite suitable for the intermediate grades as well, but may need a different approach. Chapter 12 on learning centers should be read for further detail.

Changing word problems

The chapter on modifying word problems will facilitate how well many teachers can begin differentiation. The teachers can use an anchor word problem for a specific strategy. Afterwards, that same problem could be rewritten in a variety of ways. This technique can help the struggling math students as well as challenge the students who need a different level of problems. Doing this would free the teacher to help the students who need extra assistance while the other students are busy applying their skills in different ways. On the other hand, this technique could also free the teacher to work specifically with the students who need the challenge. Changing word problems is further explained in Chapter 6.

Tiered assignments

This technique focuses on readiness skills. All of the students are instructed in essential skills, but are provided with work of different levels of difficulty. This is similar to changing the word problems. The beginning of the lesson may be the same, but the class is broken into two or three groups: below, on level, and above. The grouping is flexible and often changes from skill to skill. For the below level, students might be encouraged to use drawings and manipulatives whereas for other two levels, the word problems might entail two steps rather than one. For the above level group, the students are given more advanced versions of the same problem solving strategy.

Compacting skills

This is one of the simplest forms of differentiated instruction. There are three easy steps to compacting. Through pretesting, which can be easily administered, teachers can identify students who need instruction on required objectives from their grade levels' scope and sequence. The students, who have mastered particular objectives, are given choices of activities to work on such as anchor activities, centers, and independent projects (Reis, Burns, Renzulli, 1992). Quite often a math text will offer booklets that contain enrichment activities for each objective. Here is an opportune time for teachers to make the maximum usage of those enrichment activities. Also, there are several reproducible books geared for activities that are more complex.

Students working on these lessons must follow a few rules. While working with others on these activities, they must use a voice that carries no more than six inches. Teachers call this the **6 inch rule**. This rule keeps the noise level from interfering with instruction. The other rule is the **"speak to three"** before me. If a student is experiencing difficulty with the enrichment lesson, he must seek out three other students for help before asking the teacher. Asking other students for help is a good way to encourage students to respect each other because this strategy is very flexible. Sometimes the student who is struggling on some of the skills may actually be one of the students who can benefit from the enrichment activity. That student might be one of the "teachers" during this time.

Anchor activities

Students will complete assignments at different rates. Since this is a given, students who complete their class work must not feel as though there is nothing to do. Anchor activities are tasks that students join when they finish their class work. These activities can consist of journal writing, learning and interest centers, class projects, computer activities or other activities that students can join without teacher guidance. It is absolutely important that these activities augment student learning and not become time fillers.

The two rules explained in the previous strategy should be considered for this as well. If students need assistance with one of the activities they chose, then they should ask at least 3 other students who were also finished with their class work. Students should also follow the 6 inch rule when they need to talk to others about their work.

When teachers or parents start with differentiated instruction, they need to:

- Start small and try one particular strategy that seems to satisfy the class' needs.
- Add a little more to the strategy as the year proceeds.
- Train students to follow the two rules as well as going to the activities.
- Take the opportunity to think upon what worked and what did not.
- Plan on incorporating another strategy when they are ready.
- Determine which class would benefit the most from differentiated instruction and work on one strategy.
- Start out with two groups from the one class that needs differentiated instruction the most if applying tiered instruction.
- Take the time to explore the Internet for information on differentiated instruction
- Explain to the principal what they are planning to accomplish in case the principal might be able to locate personnel and funds that can assist the teachers.
- Take workshops and attend meetings about differentiated instruction.
- Read books on the subject.
- Find other teachers who are working this technique, share ideas, and discuss what works and what does not.

Below is an url for a website that explains the premises of differentiated instruction as well as the strategies. This particular website does a great job of explaining the various components of differentiated instruction.

http://www.eht.k12.nj.us/~jonesj/Differentiated%20Instruction/1%20DI%20Strategies.htm

Teachers should be aware of books and articles written by Carol Tomlinson. She offers a detailed look on what makes differentiated instruction important to today's classrooms. Books by Joseph Renzulli, Sally M Reis, Jann Leppien, Robert J Sternberg, and Abraham Tannenbaum can also be used to learn more about differentiated instruction.

Teachers should not think they have to accomplish everything in one year. If they do, they will become overwhelmed and might even give up on using differentiated instruction. They should find a partner or group of teachers in the same grade level and subject. Teachers need to learn to share ideas with each other. The groups could even hold meetings where they discuss what worked and what did not and why.

Teachers need to discuss their plans or goals with their principal who just might be able to find assistance in this project. For instance, Ms. Everhart discussed her plans for math with her principal. Her principal not only encouraged her to continue, but she also found resource help from the board of education to assist her. From there, Ms. Everhart and the resource teacher located other teachers from various schools on the same grade level and subject who also wanted to work on differentiating instruction. As a group, they bounced ideas off each other as well encouraged each other and discussed what was effective and motivating.

"Tell me and I'll forget; show me and I may remember; Involve me and I'll understand." Chinese proverb

Chapter 12

Problem Solving Learning Centers

Learning centers are used extensively in elementary schools for all subject matter. Some middle schools are beginning to implement learning centers as well. These learning centers provide the students the opportunity to practice skills, explore ideas, and often have fun while reviewing skills.

Since teaching problem solving skills to students in math classes require a lot of time and practice, why not utilize learning centers for the extra practice? Teachers can work with their grade level teammates. They can even share ideas with teachers from other schools. Below are some possible ideas.

In Chapter 5-Polya's 4-Step Problem Solving Model, there were worksheets provided to help teach students about some of the components of the first step-Understanding the Problem.

Why not take each component and create activities for the students to work on during center time? Some of the components from the first step that may need extra practice are:

- Finding the Question
- Rephrasing the Question in Statement Form
- Highlighting Key Words
- Determining important information that is missing
- Locating extra Information

Word problems could be written on various shapes and the students pick one of the components to work on. On the back of each shape, there could be an answer key so they can receive immediate feedback on how they did.

In an earlier chapter, there was an activity called, "Is the Answer Reasonable?" The teacher could add extra practice by creating various word problems and a solution on cards or shapes. Different shapes could represent easy to more difficult problems. Each problem could be numbered. On the back would be the answer and explanation as to why it is not reasonable. The teacher could even include problems with correct solutions to check on students' mastery of this skill.

Sudoku problems would be a great part of any problem solving center. There are various publishers and websites who create Sudoku problems just for children at different grade levels. These problems would give students extra practice on the guess and test strategy. Once again, the answer key could be on the back or have the answer key in a folder.

Logic problems, with and without the grid, can be another part of this center. There are several logic problems written for beginners, intermediate, and more advanced levels. Depending upon the ability levels and grade levels of students, there is no reason why this center cannot have a wide range of skill levels on logic problems. Answer keys should be included on the back of the card so students can obtain immediate feedback.

In Polya's 4-Step Problem Solving Model, there is the Step 2 that lists several strategies. Why not have different sections of the learning center devoted to each strategy that was introduced for each grade level? There are several reproducible books on word problems. Although most generally deal with the 4 algorithms of addition, subtraction, multiplication, and division, problems that deal with other strategies can still be found.

Have cards for:

- Draw a picture
- Guess and Test
- Use logic
- Find the pattern
- Construct a table
- Make an organized list
- Draw a diagram
- Find a similar problem
- Make the problem simpler
- Work backwards
- Write an equation

Students should be encouraged to use their problem solving journal. Perhaps one activity could be having word problems that could be classified by the strategy the student would use, or there could be several examples of word problems for each strategy. The students write down the strategy and number of the card on their paper, and then they solve the problems. For a challenge they could create their own word problems for each strategy and place them on a card with an answer key so other students can solve them.

One part of this center could be for vocabulary review for reviewing words associated with problem solving as well as other types of concepts in math. Students need to practice both areas of math terminology.

Depending upon the age/grade level of the students, the center could include the following activities:

- Matching pictures to concepts
- Matching definition to math term
- Crossword puzzle
- Classifying math terms
- Playing Go Fish
- Dominoes

There were several suggestions for vocabulary practice in Chapter 3 that could be used for learning centers.

Writing prompts concerning math should be included. The students would pick a prompt that poses a question about either problem solving in general or a particular problem. Then they would have to compose an explanation or answer to that question. The same word problems that were used in other areas of this learning center could be utilized here. For example, on the card would be a word problem. The prompt might say one of the following:

- "Why wouldn't you choose guess and test for this problem?"
- "How is this problem similar to one you have already solved in class?"
- "Justify using a calculator for this problem."

Games add spark and interest to learning centers. There are several games that deal with problem solving type activities. These games give students a taste of real world situations in a fun, competitive way. They can be played at home or at school.

Examples are:

- Allowance by Remedia Publications
- Shopping by Remedia Publications
- Real World Math by Teacher Created Resources

Challenges could be more involved word problems or projects that the gifted students could work on after they have completed their assignments. This could free the teachers so they could assist or reteach the struggling learners.

The possibilities are endless for a learning center on problem solving. It takes time to develop a learning center of any kind. If teachers have access to resource teachers, they should take advantage of that in order to design activities for this learning center. Sometimes the principals might have funds. Even the PTA might be able to assist by funding these activities.

"Expanding learning beyond the textbook both empowers students to become independent learners and exposes them to perspectives and topics they might otherwise overlook." Trisha Brummer and Stephanie Macceca

Chapter 13

Make the Connection, Motivate the Child

While teachers introduce a new story to the students in reading, they are encouraged to help the students connect with the theme, plot, or the characters in the story. Making connections to the story helps the students comprehend better as well as become more motivated to reading the story.

However, in math, connections are often omitted due to time restraints or are simply not included in the textbooks. Making connections can prove to be quite helpful and meaningful to students. Various concepts in mathematics are also interrelated rather than isolated, but that is often how these concepts are taught. The idea that mathematics is an integrated field of study is extremely important to our students' academic growth in mathematics, yet quite often, students see mathematics separated from the rest of the subjects. Seeing mathematics connected to the real world is important to motivating students to become more involved in learning about mathematical concepts.

Make Connections, Motivate the Child

This was the title of a presentation Loretta Everhart did a few years ago at an Eisenhower Conference in Maryland. She believed in it then, and still believes in it now. **Why?** Ms. Everhart discovered that the more connections she made between mathematics and other areas, the more students learned because they were motivated and involved. As often as possible, she made sure her students saw how math was interrelated with the other subjects as well as the real world.

When Ms. Everhart first started teaching, she was assigned to the fifth grade and then to sixth grade. In neither grade was the usage of manipulatives encouraged or recommended at that time. Later, this teacher was moved to third grade where manipulatives were definitely part of math instruction. Whenever Ms. Everhart employed manipulatives to teach new concepts or review ones that the students had not yet mastered, she noticed the "light bulbs" in students' heads light up. A whole new way of teaching math with the usage of those manipulatives had opened her eyes to what was missing in her lessons.

Various concepts became even clearer to the teacher from using manipulatives with the younger students. She began to wonder how much more she could have learned when she was attending school if the teachers had used manipulatives. She began to "see" how much of a visual learner she was. What a revelation that was to this teacher!

Eventually, Ms. Everhart was moved up to fifth grade again where she soon realized that being moved to third grade had helped her become a better math teacher. She decided to employ manipulatives in fifth grade just as she had in the third grade. It was amazing how well many students in the upper grades grasped difficult concepts without having to review the concepts repeatedly. As this teacher attended more math workshops and math conventions, the topic of using manipulatives in the upper elementary grades were discussed more frequently. Other people discovered as she had that manipulatives were not just for the primary grades. Now, manipulatives are even believed to be for middle grades as well.

Whenever Ms. Everhart could locate or create word problems that followed a theme, the students were more interested. Whenever she used a word problem that illustrated how the new concepts being taught were connected, the children were more attentive. Frequently she found herself searching for books that dealt with thematic units that particularly included math concepts taught in her grade. Searching for books that dealt with real world math ideas also proved to be most helpful in stimulating and motivating her students. She even started scanning the classified ads and the sales papers of the newspapers for ideas. As her students were becoming more eager to learn new skills and concepts, she found herself becoming excited about teaching again. Ms. Everhart was learning from her students that when she applied connections in her math lessons, they were more motivated and grasped the concepts more thoroughly. The connections included:

- Concrete ideas with manipulatives
- Representations with abstract ideas
- Concepts with other concepts
- Math skills with themes units
- Math skills used in science
- Math skills used in social studies
- Math skills used in language arts
- Math skills used in other subjects
- Children seeing how math is related to their real world
- Children seeing how math is related to their parents' real world
- Children being taught new skills with a word problem

Introducing skills by using a word problem

When new skills are being introduced, teachers should utilize a word problem that requires those skills. This word problem could be written on the chalkboard, smart board, chart paper, or a transparency. In groups, the students use a problem solving model to find the question. At this time, they should look for clues and necessary information and record that information on paper. After a moment of time, each group share what they found as well as discuss what strategy they should use. However they do not solve the problem at this time. Why? The teacher needs to introduce the new skill.

For example,

Introduce 2-digit addition without regrouping.

Nancy had 24 stuffed animals in her bedroom. For her birthday, her family bought her 12 more. How many does she have now?

There is no reason why the students cannot analyze the problem.

24 stuffed animals in bedroom, family bought her 12 more

The question: How many stuffed animals does she have now?

Here the teacher should explain that the students need to learn how to add two digit numbers without regrouping so they can solve problems such as the one they had just read. The problem should be posted somewhere in the classroom so the teacher can refer to it during the skill lessons. By introducing the new skill within a word problem, the teacher has demonstrated why the skill was so essential to the students. In other words, she gave the students a goal to work towards.

Concrete ideas with manipulatives

Manipulatives are not just for counting anymore. Over the years, they have become more sophisticated and useful. Base ten blocks have assisted hundreds of students in comprehending the meaning and mechanics of addition, subtraction, multiplication, and division as well as understanding place value. Fraction pieces have assisted teachers in demonstrating equivalent fractions, greater than and less than values of paired fractions, adding and subtracting of simple to complex fractions, and more. There are even fraction towers where the teacher can demonstrate how decimals and percents are related to fractions. Being able to manipulate these fractional pieces enhances the students' comprehending of fractions.

The list is endless for the vast variety of manipulatives both teacher-made and factory produced. Grade levels from Pre Kindergarten to middle school benefit from using manipulatives. Manipulatives are super tools for helping children connect concepts. These manipulatives stimulate the brain and initiate the process of learning and assimilating concepts. Manipulatives are important in assisting children in the process of learning concepts. They need manipulatives to guide them through word problems. The trick is to make time for utilizing them while instructing students since schools have been committed to timelines for the teaching and mastery of skills.

Representations with abstract ideas

One of the strategies for problem solving is using representations. Some are simple like drawing a picture or making a diagram whereas some representations like constructing a chart might take a little more time. Graphs, charts, organized lists, pictures, and diagrams are useful in helping many students organize data for predicting, generalizing, organizing, sharing, and solving.

Concepts with other concepts

Children need to see that concepts are not isolated ideas. Many are interconnected with each other. As teachers help students connect one concept with another, they are helping them understand each idea better as well as teaching them to discover the relationships of different ideas.

For example, students can use small cubes to make multiplication arrays. Then the teachers can help their students solve area problems. After all, finding the area of a rectangle is the same as finding a multiplication array. Later on, these same cubes can be organized into multiplication arrays to find prime and composite numbers. Next these cubes can form square numbers by creating multiplication arrays that are shaped like squares.

Math skills with theme units

Word problems that are related to a theme show connections and prove to students how mathematics really is not an isolated subject. Not only can many children relate well to holidays, having to solve word problems connected to a holiday becomes more meaningful and interesting. Many students also relate well to sports. Reading organized lists, interpreting graphs on teams' wins and losses as well as points earned during a game, averages, using or creating a tree diagram for team competition, and looking for patterns happen quite easily with sports data. Amazing how much math is used in so many careers. Students can investigate how various careers use math skills.

Math skills used in science

Equations and graphs are often used in science. Making predictions and generalizations are very important to both math and science. Solving for the average rainfall in a city or time lapse for a plant to grow are both considered problem solving. As the students conduct experiments, they are constructing line graphs and bar graphs so they can analyze the data and write an analysis of the results. If the class is studying flight, the students could create paper airplanes and see how far they will travel. They can measure the distance the planes traveled. Using this data, students could create a stem and leaf plot as a class and then discuss the findings. Afterwards, they could write an analysis of the findings and even predict what might occur if they alter the construction of the paper airplanes.

Math skills used in social studies

How often do students have to remember dates when they study history in school? Here is an opportunity for creating a timeline and time lapse problems. Students could construct a timeline of famous dates for American history with corresponding reports.

Population problems can also be used. Students could examine why the census is so important to our country. How is the budget important to the country as well as to each state and city? Students could write letters to the county executives to ask for information on how the budget is developed.

American currency has gone through some changes over the years. Students could research and write reports on the history of American money and coins. For students who need a challenge, research projects on foreign currency could stimulate some thinking. Students could even research on the causes of the creation of Eurocurrency.

Figuring mileage on maps is a useful skill. Using maps, the students could figure out the mileage between various cities in the United States. This could be a great opportunity for comparing the two modes of transportation, flying and driving.

Math skills used in language arts

There are so many books written for children that deal with math as a theme. Teachers could read the book, Grandfather Tang, to the students and then have the students create their own story using tangrams. Some historical novels deal with timelines. Students can work on time lapse problems. Older students could even write a story based on the American timeline. After solving a Sudoku or logic puzzle, students could be assigned the task of writing directions on how to perform either task.

Math skills used in other subjects

In gym class, the students could take their pulse before exercising. Then they could give their number to the teacher for recording. Next, the students could run in place and take their pulse reading. Once again, they could give their number to the teacher to record. Later on, the class could create a line graph for the pulse at rest and then for the pulse after exercising.

In art, teachers could locate various museums online to have the students look for geometric shapes in artwork. The students could study artists who use various figures in their abstract pictures. One example is the artwork by Mondrian. After studying his artwork, students can create their own version.

When students study geometry in grades two through five, the teacher could use the site, Greeting Card Geometry Math. The teacher can utilize this site to assist students in identifying and creating congruent and similar shapes. Later, the students can use those shapes and others to create a holiday greeting card.

In music, students could use the music section of the Online Math Applications to learn more about rhythm, pitch, frequency, and amplitude. The students can even learn how side-by-side notes on the keyboard are musically related. Also in music class, the students can learn how musical notes are related to fractions.

Children seeing how math is related to their real world

Seeing how math is related to their world is important to children's learning. One way is to have the students plan a party where they investigate what they would need to buy such as invitations, food, drinks, plastic dinnerware, prizes, and games. The teacher can control how many people should be invited and how far the party can go. This assignment could be written up in a prompt or in the form of a story problem. Because of time restraints, this project could be initiated in the classroom and the remainder could be finalized at home.

If students are investigating various states for a social studies unit, they could "prepare" a trip where they would be required to include mileage and other expenses such as food, lodging, sightseeing, and traveling. They could even write to tourist bureau of the states requesting information to enhance their project.

Children seeing how math is related to their parents' real world

Having students interview their parents to see how the adults use math in everyday life can be a powerful way to connect math to the real world. First, the students brainstorm some possible questions to ask their parents. Then the class should discuss how students should take notes. Perhaps some students who have difficulty in keeping up due to their handwriting could use a tape recorder. Some students might have access to a laptop which could be used to take notes. Possible questions for the parent interview:

• How do you use math at work?
• Can you explain that in more detail?
• How else do you use math at work and explain that in more detail.
• What are some of the ways you use math at home or around the house?
• Can you explain that in more detail?
• How else do you use math at home and explain in detail?

The students communicate their ideas to the class. To help this project become meaningful in mathematical terms, they need to include the math, not just explain it. To ensure this project is even more meaningful, the students should have the opportunity to discuss what was shared.

Results in helping students see connections in math

Providing opportunities for students to see how math is connected to other concepts, other subjects, their world and the world of the adults in their lives will:

- Open the students' minds to math
- Increase learning
- Motivate students to do their best
- Capture their interests in math
- Realize that math and math concepts are not in an isolated world.
- Alleviate students' fear in math
- Help some of the students choose math for their career.

"You have to take enough time to get kids deeply involved in something they can think about in lots of different ways." Howard Gardner

Summary

Teaching children how to solve word problems can start as soon as they start reading, whether the reading is done by them or by their parents. Starting early with literature and games can motivate children to learn more about using problem solving in their world.

Adults need to be aware of math anxiety and how students might exhibit signs of math anxiety in class. They should keep in mind that sometimes a teacher's method of teaching math can lead to math anxiety. Also, children can develop math anxiety by how the parents communicate their fears or expectations to them.

Both teachers and parents need to be aware of various learning styles so they can adapt math lessons accordingly to meet the needs of the children. Using reading and writing strategies can assist the students with mastering math vocabulary and communicating ideas in math class. Modeling and math talk can also lead to more productive learning. Whenever possible, cooperative learning and differentiating instruction should be part of lesson planning.

Having a copy of a problem solving model on hand for the children to use while they solve word problems can assist them in being organized. Being organized is extremely important in order for children to become comfortable with mathematics. Polya's Problem Solving Model is one example of a problem solving model that is used nationwide. Some school sytems have adapted that model to suit the educational philosophy being observed by those schools. Singapore Math employs another style, but the whole school needs to adopt it in order for the students to become comfortable and adept at using such a model. The Internet is a great resource for locating various problem solving models. Teachers and parents need to ensure they familiarize their students with the various strategies used in problem solving such as finding a pattern, drawing a picture, using logic, and using an equation.

Keeping a well organized math binder that includes a word problem journal and a vocabulary section can assist the students in the classroom as well as at home.

Practicing math vocabulary is very important if children are to comprehend and solve more difficult word problems. Having a word problem journal can help children when they forget how to use a specific strategy. Being able to review the journal can help children feel more comfortable with problem solving.

Using real word application whenever possible can help the students connect math to their world, thus making math meaningful and interesting. Word problems can be adapted so students can practice their skills. Modifying word problems can help the adults make the most of the word problems. However, students should be given the opportunity to practice each type of modified problem.

Learning to be good, effective problem solvers can lead to promising careers later on in life. Learning to be good, effective problem solvers can help students become adept at solving problems they encounter in real life. Problem solving skills are indeed important.

Appendix

Permission to photocopy the student activities and charts in the Appendix of this book is hereby granted to one teacher or parent as part of the purchase price. This permission may only be used to provide copies for this teacher's or parent's instructional setting. This permission may not be transferred, sold, or given to any additional or subsequent users of this book. Reproduction for an entire school, school district, or for commercial use is prohibited.

Websites for Teachers, Parents, and Children

Below are some various websites that can either be used with children or give teachers and parents further information on problem solving. The adults should always check out the websites before they permit the children to use them.

Calculation Nation is a game site for upper elementary to middle school age students. It is sponsored by the NCTM, a national association for mathematics teachers. Some of the skills are fractions, symmetry, factors, and more. It is free to join, but you do need to sign in. There is a category for parents and teachers where they can obtain more information on each game.

http://calculationnation.nctm.org/Games/Default.aspx

Kidzone has worksheets for each grade level on math skills and word problems. The word problems are fixed so each time someone clicks on them, the word problem may be the same, but the numbers are different. So if any of the students have math anxiety about word problems, the sameness might have help give them the confidence to persevere.

http://www.kidzone.ws/math/wordproblems.htm

Math Playground has games, logic puzzles, word problems, and videos that adults and the students can view for free. There are neat activities for involving students of all levels of abilities. The tangram activity does not really involve the 7 tangrams and can be difficult to manipulate, but the other games and activities seem to be motivating.

http://www.mathplayground.com/wordproblems.html

For **ixl** website, there are various grade levels from Kindergarten to grade 6. Teachers click on the grade level they want their students to use. Then they click on the skill they want them to practice. This is an interactive site where children are asked to solve a problem and type in their answer. When they click on submit they are told whether or not their answer is correct. They also have the opportunity to click on Explanation which seems to be easy to understand and thorough for the particular problem. Adults do need to register, but it seems to be free.

This is a great site for home schoolers, children practicing at home, computer lab in school or in the classroom, or whole classroom participation.

http://www.ixl.com/

Aplusmath has a section that can help adults create flash cards for children. There are also math games that children can play for skill strengthening. There is advertising, so teachers and parents need to look this site over and decide what part they want the children to use.

http://www.aplusmath.com/

Super Kids offers math worksheets for free. The skills can be simple addition or complex division. Parents and teachers determine how many problems will be on the page as well as the math skill.

Also, there is a section on logic and reasoning. This is a small collection of classic games that require children to challenge their minds. These games focus on spatial reasoning and strategy. Examples are Battleship, Sorter, Breakout, and Towers of Hanoi.

http://www.superkids.com/aweb/tools/

Helping Your Child Learn Math is a free site from the US Department of Education. This site has many activities for parents to do with their children to spark that interest in math. It even gives pointers to parents. There are also articles for parents to read.

http://www2.ed.gov/pubs/parents/Math/index.html

Home School Math is a website that lists other websites that offer a variety of activities and information on problem solving skills

http://www.homeschoolmath.net/online/problem_solving.php

Hoodamath.com is a website that has worksheets, games, and tutorials. Parents and teachers should look over this site to make sure it is appropriate for their children.

http://www.hoodamath.com/worksheets/

Then there are some websites that offer teachers and parents great choices of worksheets and activities that delve into the world of problem solving. Some are free while others charge a yearly membership fee. Some have quite a variety of word problems that can be used.

TLSBooks.com offers free worksheets for all subjects, not just math. There seems to be quite a variety of math skills covered on this site. There are two math games. Both teachers and parents can use this site to give their children additional practice or challenge.

http://www.tlsbooks.com/mathworksheets.htm

Math Stories.com is for both teachers and parents who want extra word problems. The fee is about $26 per year, but if a school wants to use this site, the fee would be different. There are open-ended problems, thematic problems, and critical thinking problems. All of which follow NCTM guidelines. For grades 1-6

http://www.mathstories.com/

EdHelper.com has a variety of math worksheets as well as word problems for parents and teachers to use. There are also puzzles that can be printed and used to challenge students. There is a fee to join which is good for a year. However, there is such wide selection with answer keys, that both parents and teachers might find this site worth the price.

http://www.edhelper.com/

The Logic Puzzles website is free and has various levels from Very Easy to Very Difficult. The puzzles can be printed. Great to help the adults find some logic and lateral puzzles to create a learning center on puzzles.

http://www.folj.com/puzzles/

In **Puzzlers Paradise**, some of the puzzles are free and seem easy to print. They seem to be appropriate for intermediate students.

http://www.puzzlersparadise.com/index.html

ABC Teach has a few free worksheets that adults can use, but if parents and teachers want to try their other worksheets, there is a yearly fee. Some of the activities came up without any difficulty. There are no answer keys provided with the free worksheets, but answer keys are provided when the yearly fee is paid. These activities are written by teachers for teachers but parents will find this site convenient as well.

http://abcteach.com/directory/basics/math/problem_solving/

About Math is really for teachers and parents to use to locate information on teaching various math skills as well as finding worksheets. Some people may find the ads objectionable for students to see, but they are not part of the worksheets.

http://math.about.com/od/wordproblem1/Worksheets_for_Word_Problems_Various_grades.htm

Polya's 4-Step Problem Solving Model

Step 1 Understand the Problem

Step 2 Develop a plan to solve the problem

Step 3 Carry out the plan

Step 4 Look back

Polya's 4 Step Problem Solving Model

1. Understanding the problem

- Read the problem.
- Do you understand the problem?
- Reread the problem if you don't understand it.
- Can you rephrase the problem in a statement?
- Highlight key words.
- What are you trying to solve or find out?
- What are the unknowns?
- What information did you find in the problem?
- What information is missing?
- What information is not needed?

2. Develop a plan to solve the problem

- Draw a picture
- Write an equation
- Use guess and check
- Look for a pattern
- Examine related problems to see if the same strategy can be used or applied
- Examine a simpler case of the problem for further understanding
- Make a table
- Make a diagram
- Work backwards
- Identify a subgoal-Some problems may have more than one step
- Make an organized list

3. Carry out the Plan

- Use one or more of the strategies from Step 2
- Decide on what tools you will need to carry out your plan
- Check each step of the plan as you work.
- Keep an accurate record of your work.

4. Looking Back

- Check the results
- Does your answer make sense?
- Is your answer reasonable?
- Rework your problem if necessary or use another strategy

Name _____ Date _____

Finding the Question

When you have word problems to solve, the first step is to decide what the problem is asking you to do. Find the question, but you must use your own words.

1. Some word problems only have one sentence.
How much money do you owe when you buy three candy bars at $.50 each?

The question asks

2. Some word problems have two sentences. One sentence has the information you need to solve the problem. The other one has the question.

Tomas bought a shirt for $12.85 at The Clothing Mart and then he bought a shirt for $14.97 at The Shirt Mart. How much more did the shirt from The Shirt Mart cost than the shirt from The Clothing Mart?

The question asks

3. There are word problems that have two sentences where each one has important information for solving the problem.
The Game Shop sells computer games for $15.75 each. If Allen has a $50 gift certificate, how many games can he buy?

The question asks

4. The question sometimes might not have a question mark.
At the Game Shop, the computer games normally sell for $15.75 each, but today they are 20% off. Find out how much each game costs with the sale.

The question asks

Rephrasing the Question in Statement Form.

Read each problem. Find the question. Then rephrase the question in statement form. Leave a blank in the statement for the answer.

1. Bria 's birthday was today and she wanted to celebrate it with her classmates in school. She decided to bring 96 Willy Wonka candy bars to give to her 24 classmates. How many candy bars will each classmate receive if Bria distributes them equally?

2. Terrence rode on the subway in the city quite frequently to go to various places. He rode on the Yellow Line 72 times last year. During that same year, he rode the Red Line 48 times more than he did the Yellow Line. How many times did Terrance ride on the Red Line last year?

3. The train from Stansfield to Eldersville makes 789 stops along the route. The same train continues from Eldersville to Miden Heights with 43 stops. How many stops altogether does this train make?

4. Mr. Bee baked cinnamon cookies for the school's bake sale. He decided to put 3 cookies in each bag. If he had 12 bags, how many cinnamon cookies did he bake for the bake sale?

5. Last year, Mr. Bee baked 48 chocolate chip cookies for the school's bake sale. How many more cookies did he bake last year than he baked this year?

Key Words for the Four Operations

If you are working on word problems that work well with equations or using the algorithms, identifying key words or phrases can help. However, keep in mind that not every problem will contain these word problems.

AdditionSubtraction

How many	How much more
Altogether	Which is more
Combine	By how much
Total	Difference
Sum	Remove
How much	Decreased by
Increased by	Minus
Together	Less
Added to	Less than
Both	Fewer than
In all	How many more
Additional	Left
Another	Remain
Raise	Take away
Perimeter	Dropped, Lost, Fell

Words ending in er such as heavier, taller, smaller, lighter, faster, slower, farther, higher, lower . . . usually signify subtraction

Multiplication	Division
Product	Share
Total	Distribute
Area	Quotient
Times	Average
Multiplied	Equally
Increased by	In each
Decreased by	Per
Percent	Separate . . . equally
Factor	Ratio
Every	Percent
At this rate	Split
Each	Equal pieces
Doubled,	Tripled, or Quadrupled Cut
As much	

Name _____ Date _____

Is the Answer Reasonable?

For each problem, think about the answer. Is it reasonable? Explain your answer.

1. Susie eats five cookies a day. How many cookies would she eat in a week?

    $5 \times 7 = 30$ cookies

2. There are 596 students in the choir. The band has 237 fewer students than the choir. How many students are in the band?

    596

    +237

    833 students

3. David spent $96.73 on a pack of hockey cards at the card show. His dad spent $61.58 on a pack of soccer cards. How much did David and his dad spend altogether?

$96.73 + $61.58 = $1,583. 10

4. Atticus has $90 from washing windows. He bought basketball shoes that cost $76.95 and a pair of socks that cost $7.96. How much money does he have left?

$76.95 $90.00

+ 7.96   −84.91

$84.91 $5.09

5. There were 41 students playing soccer during recess. Eighteen were girls. How many were boys?

    18–41 = 37 boys

6. There were three teams playing during recess. The Red Team scored 18 points. The Blue team scored 5 more points than the Red Team. The Blue Team scored how many points?

    3 + 18 + 5 = 26 points

7. The library lent 8,545 books in the first marking period. In the second marking period, it lent over 6,000 books. How many more books did they lend in the first marking period than the second marking period?

6,000

– 8,545

2,455 more books

8. There are 165 people waiting to ride on a roller coaster. If only 5 people can ride on the roller coaster at a time, how many rides does the roller coaster have to complete in order for each person waiting to get a ride?

165 / 5 = 31 rides

9. Ramona paid $58.86 for 6 pounds of shrimp for a party. How much does the shrimp cost per pound?

$58.86

x 6

$353.16

10. The zookeeper uses fresh hay each day in the elephants' stalls. He uses 5 bales of hay for each elephant stall. If there are 20 stalls, how many bales of hay does he need for one day? How many bales of hay does he need for 1 week?

5 x 20 = 100 bales of hay for one day

1 x 100 = 100 bales of hay for the week

Check List for Step 3

In order for me to check my work and make sure it is accurate, I need to do the following:

- Write down the type of strategy that I am using.
- Make sure my work is neat.
- Be organized.
- If I must erase a part, then I must do it carefully.
- Leave spaces behind each portion of a problem.
- Leave spaces behind each problem so they don't run into each other as I recheck my work.
- List tools that I used other than a pencil and paper.
- Ask myself, "When I look over my work, will I be able to understand my own work?"
- Ask myself, "When my teacher or parent look over my work, will they be able to understand my work so they can help me and grade my work?"

Scanning the Passage

Scanning is a useful tool for rereading the passage. As you read each problem, you need to ask yourself the following questions to help you understand the passage.

- what do I understand
- what is not clear to me
- why it is not clear to me
- what is the problem
- what needs to be done in order to solve the problem
- what do I need in order to do that
- what information is given
- what information is missing
- which details are not needed

Coding the Text

The codes:

?	I am confused/I don't understand
M	I want to learn more about this
*	This is important
N	New information
C	Connection
TH	Theme of the text
AHA	Big idea in the text

Writing Prompts

Problem #1

Marjorie made a sandwich for her lunch at work. She used two slices of bread at 65 calories each. She spread 1 tablespoon of margarine at 101 calories. Next she added 1 slice of cheese at 101 calories and a slice of meat at 161 calories. How many calories were in her sandwich?

Prompt 1

If someone solved the problem with an answer of 49 calories, would that answer make sense? Explain your answer.

Prompt 2

How do you find the number of calories for the two slices of bread being used in the above problem?

Prompt 3

Write the question in a statement form.

Writing Prompts

Problem #2

Two sisters went to a rock concert last night. The concert lasted from 8:00 P.M. until 11:30 P.M. that night. If the feature band played on the stage for 2 hours and 15 minutes, how much of the total concert time did the band not play?

Prompt #1

How long was the concert and how did you find the answer?

Prompt #2

How many minutes did the feature band play that night? Explain your answer.

Prompt #3

Restate the question in a statement form.

Prompt #4

How would you solve the problem? Why?

Prompt #5

Which problem solving strategy would you use to solve the problem and why?

Writing Prompts

Problem #3

The odometer on the family car read 39,871 when the family took a day trip. They left 5:30 A.M. that morning and did not return home until 8:30 P.M. the same day. When they returned home, the odometer read 40,082. How many miles did the family use for the day trip?

Prompt #1

Was there any data not needed to answer the question? Explain your answer.

Prompt #2

If the car used 25 miles per gallon, how many gallons of gasoline were needed for this day trip? How do you know?

Prompt #3

If gasoline cost $2.57 a gallon, how much did the family spend on gasoline for this day trip? Do you have enough information in the above problem to answer that question? Why or why not?

Name _____ Date _____

Missing Information or Too Much Information

You are to change each problem so that one is missing key information and another one has too much information.

1a. Mr. Jackson's students will walk to the picnic area with adult chaperones. He has 25 students and 5 adults. He assigned one of the parents to help him carry the drinks while two other parents carried the treats. How many groups of students will be walking to the picnic area?

1b.

2a. For the class picnic, Mr. Jackson bought juice boxes that come 4 to a package, five large bags of pretzels, and five boxes of treats that come 5 to a box. If each person drinks one juice box, how many packages of juice boxes will Mr. Jackson need to buy so everyone on the picnic will have something to drink?

2b.

Drawing a Picture

The school library held a book sale. Carla bought 3 books. Then her mother came in to the sale and bought Carla 6 books. How many books does she have now?

Writing an Equation

1. Shawn and Brea bought lunch at the card show. Brea spent $9.75 on a tuna sandwich and a soda. Shawn spent $12.40 on a hamburger, fries, and a soda. How much less did Brea spend on lunch than Shawn?

2. Brian built a bookcase with three shelves. If he can fit 10 books, all of which are the same size, in the first shelf, what would the total number of books he could possibly fit in the whole bookcase if the remaining books are the same size as the ones on the first shelf?

3. This summer Marybeth bought 34 tiny stuffed animals for her bedroom. Yesterday, she gave seventeen of them to her friend. How many does she have now?

4. The art teacher was preparing for school. She bought 30 boxes of crayons. Each box had 24 crayons. Each box costs $.35. How much did she spend on those crayons?

Working Backwards

Tommy, Donnie, and Bonnie are three of Dr. Samson's children. Tommy is 3 years older than Donnie. Bonnie is 15 years old and is 5 years older than Tommy. How old is Donnie?

Guess and Test

Activity	Costs
Miniature Golf	$3.50
Skating	$2.50
Go-Kart Rides	$2.75
Skate Boarding	$3.25
Ping-Pong	$2.25

Tomas decided to go to Fun World where there are various activities children of all ages can do. He picked two of the activities from a chart of 5. He paid with a ten dollar bill. He received $4 as his change. Which two activities did he get involved in? Was that the only answer to this problem? Show your work.

Identify Subgoals

Maria loves shopping. She loves to shop so much that she drives to the Senator Mall once a week. Two weeks ago, Maria visited seven stores, but only made purchases at two. First, Maria went to Music City, a place that specializes in all items of music. She browsed for 2 hours before making a decision on what to buy. At the checkout counter, she had 3 CDs that were priced at $10.99 each and 1 second hand CD priced at $5.95. During this time, she gave the sales associate 2 twenty dollar bills. How much change should she receive? Show your work.

Next, Maria went to Girls' Boutique where she tried on five blouses, three skirts, and eight necklaces. After some careful thinking, she decided on three blouses which cost $21.99, $18.50, and $26.99. She also bought two skirts which cost $35.99 each. How much money did she spend at this store? Show your work.

Explain how you solved this problem.

Shopping made Maria hungry so she stopped at the Blue Jay Inn where she met her friend, Holly. After the two of them read the menu posted outside the restaurant, they decided to go in. Maria ordered a salad at $5.75, a deluxe cheeseburger at $8.99, and an ice tea for $1.50. Holly picked the crab cake sandwich for $9.50, fries at $1.50, and a soda for $2.50.

Who spent more for their lunch and by how much?

Did you add, subtract, multiply, or divide to find your answer? Why?

Finding Patterns

Nancy's family room floor is done in square tiles. She was noticing how the small squares can form larger squares. As Nancy studied these different size squares she discovered there were patterns in the perimeters and areas of those squares. What patterns in the squares' perimeters and areas do you think she might have found? How should you prove your answer? Show your work.

Can Nancy use those patterns to predict what the perimeters and areas of even larger squares would be? How do you know?

Making an Organized List

Mrs. Jackson bought some pants and shirts for her son, Jacob. She bought 4 pants-black, brown, blue, and tan. She also purchased 5 shirts-white, yellow, red, purple, and light blue. How many different outfits can Jacob make with those 4 pants and 5 shirts? What are the different outfits?

Making a Table

Mr. Danver has a landscaping business called The Green Thumb. His son, Rudy, was collecting data on how many jobs the business had each month from March to September.

Rudy's data was: March-20; April-55; May-70; June-65; July-55; August-35; September-70

Construct a table for Rudy's data collection. Next, use the information to construct a bar graph. After carefully studying both the table and the graph, think about why each month had a certain number of jobs. Did March have the fewest because not everyone was ready for planting? At first, there was plenty of rain, but one month there was a drought. Which do you think there must have been a drought and why do you think that? Why do you think there were plenty of jobs for May and June?

Then write an analysis of the findings. In that analysis figure out which month there was a drought, which month people wanted their gardens prepared for the winter, and which months were the busiest because The Green Thumb was planting flowers. Explain your answers.

Also, in the analysis, predict what the table and bar graph might look like for next year and explain why you think that.

Using Logic

There are five people in the Everhart family. They are Russell, Jean, John, Paul, and Mary. Their ages are 12, 20, 21, 39, and 45. Russell is the oldest member while Jean is the youngest member of this family. John is 8 years older than Jean. Paul is not 45. How old is Mary?

Construct a chart to help you sort through the clues.

Using a Diagram

In a classroom of 45 students, 38 said they loved art and 27 said they loved music. Twenty-two students said that they loved both subjects. How many students in the classroom do not like either subject?

Draw two intersecting circles and one small one to help you solve this problem. Make sure you label each circle.

Which Strategy?

In September, the fourth grade had a book reading contest. Steven read 9 books, Allen read 5, Cierra read 8, Kristen read 11, Mary read 3, and Marcus read 6. Who read the most books, the girls or the boys?

Bobby gave three of his baseball cards to his cousin. He started with 35. How many does he have now?

Maria's Shopping Adventures

Maria went to Music City, a place that specializes in all items of music. She browsed for 2 hours before making a decision on what to buy. At the checkout counter, she had 3 CDs that were priced at $10 each and 1 second hand CD priced at $5. During this time, she gave the sales associate two twenty dollar bills. How much change should Maria receive from the cashier?

Maria went to Music City, a place that specializes in all items of music. She browsed for 2 hours before making a decision on what to buy. At the checkout counter, she had 4 CDs that were priced at $10.98 each and 2 second hand CDs priced at $5.95 a piece. During this time, she gave the sales associate 3 twenty dollar bills. How much change should Maria receive from the cashier?

Maria went to Computer Land where people can find all sorts of computer games. She wanted to get her brother some games for his birthday. Since her brother loves sports, she bought 2 sports games at $32.85 a piece. If she gave the cashier $100, how much money would she have left?

Maria went to Computer Land where people can find all sorts of computer games at various prices. She wanted to buy some games for her brother's birthday. Since he loves sports, she decided to check into games with sports as the theme. She found two different price levels. One set of sports games was selling for $24.95 each. The second group of games was selling for $32.85 a piece. Maria wanted to find out how many games she could buy for $100. Figure out the combinations of sports games at the two prices. Remember, her total cannot be over $100. She could be just under, but not over. You also need to remember that she was buying games under two different price categories.

Maria went to Computer Land where people can find all sorts of computer games. She wanted to get her brother some games for his birthday. Since her brother loves sports, she bought some sports games at $32.85 a piece. When she gave the cashier $100, she received $34.30. How many games did she buy? Construct a table to help you find the possibilities.

Maria went to Music City, a place that specializes in all items of music. She browsed for 2 hours before making a decision on what to buy. At the checkout counter, she had 4 CDs that were priced at $10.98 each and 2 second hand CDs priced at $5.95 a piece. During this time, she gave the sales associate 3 twenty dollar bills.

How much money did the cashier give her?

Maria went to Music City, a place that specializes in all items of music. She browsed for 2 hours before making a decision on what to buy. At the checkout counter, she had 5 CDs that were priced at $15.50 each and 3 second hand CDs priced at $5.95 a piece. Maria has $95 in her handbag.

How much money will Maria's choices cost altogether? Show your work. What might Maria do with her choices in order to afford them? Explain your answer.

Construct a table to show the different possibilities of purchasing CDs priced at $15.50 and CDs priced at $5.95. The total cannot be more than $95. Write about the choices that Maria can make.

Picturing in One's Mind

Tom was watching birds that came to the backyard feeder. He kept track of how many he saw each day. For Sunday, Tom saw 12 birds, 1 squirrel, and one cat come to the bird feeder. On Monday, he saw 5 birds. Tuesday, he saw 8 birds and one cat. Then on Wednesday, he spotted 8 more birds and three squirrels. For Thursday and Friday, he noticed that 6 birds came each day. He also saw 2 squirrels during each of those two days. Last, he recorded 9 birds for Saturday.

How many birds did Tom see during that week?

Breaking Down the Problem into Smaller Parts

Problem: John has a target board made out of vinyl material. There were three balls made of sticky material like that found on Velcro fasteners. On the target there are three ways to score. In the center there is a 2" square made out of Velcro. That square is worth 100 points. On the outside there are pink circles and large green squares. The 4 pink circles are worth 50 points. The smaller green squares are worth 20 points.

Find the highest score using 3 balls. Then find the lowest score using 3 balls. Each time, all of the balls were attached to the target.

How many combinations of scoring can you find? Make a chart to show the combinations. Show your work.

Using Manipulatives

Sara was visiting the local pond with her dad. At the pond were several ducks. Swimming in the pond were five ducks. Walking around the rim of the pond were 8 ducks. Then two feet away were 7 ducks looking for food. How many ducks did Sara see? Show your work.

Write an explanation about how you solved the problem.

Role Playing the Problem

Maria wants to plan a garden of flowers for the backyard. She thinks a garden of 5 feet by 8 feet would be a good size. However, she needs to prepare the ground by adding rich topsoil. How much topsoil would she need to buy if she digs up the ground 5 feet by 8 feet by 3 inches deep? What information is needed in order to solve this problem?

Bibliography

Bell, N. & Tuley, K. (2002). *On cloud nine.* San Luis Obispo, CA: Gander Educational Publishing

Brandenburg, M.L. (2002). *Advanced math? Write! Educational Leadership*, 60 (3), 67-68.

Brummer, T. & Macceca, S. (2004). Reading strategies for mathematics. Shell Education.

Burns, M. (2007). *Nine ways to catch kids up.* Educational Leadership. Retrieved from: http://www.mathsolutions.com/documents/2007_Nine_Ways.pdf

Burns, M. (1995). *Writing in math class?* Absolutely! *Instructor*, 104 (7), 40-47.

Burns, M. (2004). *Writing in math. Educational Leadership*, 62 (2), 30-33.

Capps, L.R. (1989, April). *Problem solving: Is language a problem?* Paper present at the annual meeting of the National Council of Teachers of Mathematics, Orlando, FL.

Chamot, A. U. & O'Malley, J. M. (1994). *The CALLA Handbook: Implementing the Cognitive Academic Language Learning Approach.* New York: Addison-Wesley Publishing Company, Inc.

Clawson, C.C. (1991). *Conquering math phobia: A painless primer.* John Wiley and Sons.

Evans, C. S. (1984). *Writing to learn in math. Language Arts*, 61, 828-35.

Fortescue, C. M. (1994). *Using oral and written language to increase understanding of math concepts. Language Arts*, 71, 578-80.

Forsten, C. (1992). *Teaching thinking and problem solving in math: Strategies, problems, and activities.* New York, NY: Scholastic Professional Books.

Fotoples, R.M. (2000). *Overcoming math anxiety.* Kappa Delta Pi Record, 36 (4), 149-151.

Indiana Department of Education. (2006). *Indiana's academic standards: High school mathematics. IDEANet*. Retrieved from: http://dc.doe.in.gov/Standards/AcademicStandards/StandardSearch.aspx

Jackson, CD & Leffingwell RJ. (1999). *The role of instructors in creating math anxiety in students from kindergarten through college*. Mathematics Teacher, 92 (7), 583-586.

Kang, H. & Pham K. T. (1995). *From 1 to Z: Integrating math and language learning*. Long Beach, CA: Teachers of English to Speakers of Other Languages. (ERIC Document Reproduction Service No. ED 381 031)

Kogelman, S. Dr. & Warren, J. Dr. (1979). *Mind over math: Put yourself on the road to success by freeing yourself from math anxiety*. McGraw-Hill

McGehe, C. A. (1991). *Mathematics the write way. Instructor*, 100 (8), 36-38.

Miller, D. (1997). *Problem solving explorations*. New York, NY: Macmillan Publishing Company.

Mitchell, R. (1996). *Contemporary's breakthrough in math: Developing problem-solving skills*. Chicago, IL: NTC/Contemporary Publishing Group, Inc.

National Council of Teachers of Mathematics. (2006). *Principles and standards for school math*. Retrieved October 30, 2006 standards.nctm.org/document/appendix/process.htm#bp3

Nitert, C. (1996). *Problem solving with math: Selecting successful strategies*. Rowley, MA: Didax

Panchyshyn, R. (1995, Dec.). *Vocabulary considerations for teaching mathematics*. Childhood Education. Retrieved from: http://www.thefreelibrary.com/_/print/PrintArticle.aspx?id=17837737

Pugalee, D. K., DiBiase, W. J. & Wood, K. D. (1999). *Writing and the development of problem solving in mathematics and science. Middle School Journal* 30(5), 48-52.

Reis, S., Burns, D., and Renzulli, J. (1992). *Curriculum compacting*. Mansfield, CT: Creative Learning Press.

Renzulli, J. S. , Leppein, J. H., and Hays, T. S. (2000). *The multiple menu model: A practical guide for developing differentiated curriculum*. Mansfield, CT: Creative Learning Press.

Schiffman, H. (1997). *Linguistic register*. Retrieved November 11, 2006 ccat.sas.upenn.edu/~haroldfs/messeas/regrep/node2.html

Sherman, H.J., Richardson, L.I., & Yard, G.J. (2009). *Teaching learners who struggle with mathematics: systematic intervention and remediation*, 2/E. Allyn & Bacon.

Silbey, R. (2005). *Math out loud! heard the word? talking and writing about math boosts understanding in a big way.* Instructor.

Sousa, D.A., (2008). *How the brain learns mathematics.* Thousand Oaks,CA: Corwin Press.

Stuart, V.B. (2000). *Math curse or math anxiety?* Teaching Children Mathematics, 6 (5), 330-335.

Tamarkin, K. (2000). *Contemporary's number power: A real world approach to math.* Chicago, IL: Wright Group/McGraw-Hill.

Tichnor, M.S. & Jewell, M. J. (2001). *Using e-mail to write about math. The Educational Forum 65* (4), 300-308.

Tobias, S., (1993). *Overcoming math anxiety.* W.W. Norton & Company.

Tomlinson, C. A (1999). *The differentiated classroom: Responding to the needs of all learners.* Alexandria, VA: Association for Supervision and Curriculum Development.

Tomlinson, C. A, and Eidson, C. C. (2003). *Differentiation in practice: A resource guide for differentiating curriculum.* Alexandria, VA: Association for Supervision and Curriculum Development.

Winebrenner, S. (1992, 2001). *Teaching gifted kids in the regular classroom.* Minneapolis, MN: Free Spirit Publishing.

Zaccaro, E. (2006). *Becoming a problem solving genius: A handbook of math strategies.* Hickory Grove Press.

Zaslavsky, C. (1996). *Fear of math: How to get over it and get on with your life.* Rutgers University Press.

Notes